Pushkin's *Evgenii Onegin*

S. Dalton-Brown

Bristol Classical Press

Critical Studies in Russian Literature

First published in 1997 by
Bristol Classical Press
an imprint of
Gerald Duckworth & Co. Ltd
The Old Piano Factory
48 Hoxton Square, London N1 6PB

A catalogue record for this book is available from the British Library

ISBN 1-85399-473-1

Available in USA and Canada from:
Focus Information Group
PO Box 369
Newburyport
MA 01950

Printed in Great Britain by
Booksprint, Bristol

Contents

Acknowledgements

My thanks go to Neil Cornwell for suggesting the idea to me, and to Mike Pursglove for pointing out certain obvious omissions, and for allowing his proof-reading skills to be ruthlessly exploited during preparation of the script; both gentlemen very kindly brought several overlooked references to my attention. Any errors or absences remaining are indisputably my own.

Introduction: 'An encyclopaedia of Russian life?'[1]

The plot of Pushkin's most famous and best-loved work, *Evgenii Onegin*, is, it has been said, absurdly simple: girl meets boy, boy rejects girl, then meets girl later and falls in love with her; girl, who is now married, rejects boy. This summary, one which omits the major event of Lenskii's death at Onegin's hand, does not, of course, do any justice whatsoever to a text which has long baffled and which continues to baffle critics. It has in fact offered a rather misleading view of the text, as one of distinctive patterning and symmetry. As Gukovskii has argued, there appear to be two mirroring situations in the text. Onegin and Tat'iana are introduced, she falls in love, writes him a letter and they meet; she 'trembles and is silent. he makes a didactic and unfair speech, though one marked by honesty and warmth. At this point the line breaks off' (Gukovskii, 1957: 271). This situation is followed by a repetition; Onegin and Tat'iana are reintroduced, he falls in love and writes her a letter; they meet. 'He trembles and is silent. She makes a speech, of the kind he had made earlier. Here the line breaks off; the novel is over' (Gukovskii, 1957: 272).[2]

Such symmetry tantalises and deludes, for there are no neat patterns which explain the text in its entirety. Scholars are still in search of the elusive formula which will allow for a unified textual reading, and which might include to a greater or lesser degree all the myriad possibilities implicit in the work. Belinskii's famous formulation of this novel in verse as an 'encyclopaedia of Russian life', despite its assumption that the text is primarily realistic, suggests the great mass of ideas, impressions, thoughts and possibilities to be found in this text, which could perhaps be read like an encyclopaedia, albeit a rather eccentrically compiled one. Belinskii may have been closer to the mark than he knew, for this study adopts the general line that the text is about knowledge, ways of gaining knowledge, and the frustration of 'not knowing'. In *Evgenii Onegin*, a novel very much about the impossibility of freedom, ignorance offers 'possibility' – the many possible ways of interpreting the text – as the only freedom.

Apart from this approach, which focusses on the themes of knowledge and freedom, the reader will find outlined in this study various other pathways towards understanding the multifaceted nature of *Evgenii Onegin*. After an overview of the critical literature written on the novel to date in Part I, Part II offers a chapter-by-chapter summary intended to familiarise the reader with all the significant aspects of each section of the work. The study concludes in Part III with a series of 'readings' of the novel, isolated according to the textual aspect on which each reading focusses, such as the question of genre, or the function of the narrator, for example. In terms of secondary sources which will allow the reader to expand his comprehension of certain points omitted for reasons of space or clarity, the emphasis is on critical studies of the novel written in either Russian or English, which will be most accessible to the reader.[3]

Notes to Introduction

1. This famous phrase was coined by Vissarion Belinskii. See his *Polnoe sobranie sochinenii* (Moscow, Izd. Ak. Nauk, 1953-9), VII, p. 503.

2. Nabokov also suggests that chapter VIII 'echoes' Chapter I. See his *Eugene Onegin* (Princeton, Princeton University Press, 1975), I, 6.

3. There are, of course, very many general works on Pushkin's life and work. One useful starting point for the reader is *Russian Views of Pushkin* (ed, trans. D.J. Richards and C.R.S. Cockrell) (Oxford, Meeuws, 1976). Although it only contains two detailed references to *Onegin*, it does include 25 translated articles on the poet, from Gogol (1834) to Blagoi (1968). See in particular Pisarev's and Dostoevskii's comments (pp. 55-60; 77-82).

Part One: Criticism

The reader with a particular interest in the history of critical approaches to the novel is directed to the following works: V. Zelinskii's seven-part compilation, *Russkaia kriticheskaia literatura o proizvedeniiakh A.S. Pushkina* (1887-1903), an invaluable guide to 19th-century criticism; J. Douglas Clayton's *Ice and Flame* (1985), the first chapter of which, although now ten years out of date, contains useful detail on some aspects of the critical history offered below, and S. Hoisington's *Russian Views of Pushkin's 'Eugene Onegin'* (1988), which contains translations of several of the major articles referred to below. Also of use are B. van Sambeek-Weideli's *Die russische Rezeption von Pushkins Evgenii Onegin* (1989), which offers a history of critical approaches, concentrating chiefly on the 19th century, and which includes a useful listing of dissertations on *Onegin* published between 1940 and 1982; B. S. Meilakh's 'Spory o Evgenii Onegine v proshlom i nastoiashchem' in his *Talisman. Kniga o Pushkine* (1975), pp. 239-302; and I. Usok's 'Roman A.S. Pushkina Evgenii Onegin i ego vospriiatie v Rossii XIX-XX v.', in *Russkaia literatura v istoriko-funktsial'nom osveshchenii* (1979).

Nineteenth-century Russian criticism

Pushkin did not expect the appearance of *Evgenii Onegin* to be greeted calmly; his experience of contemporaries' critical talents had not inclined him towards complacency; and, after all, the rewards of fame are 'nonsensical talk, noise and abuse' ('krivye tolki, shum i bran'!', *Onegin*, I: 60). In 1825, in the initial Foreword to Chapter I (which he dropped when the novel was published in its entirety), Pushkin addressed his critics. He suggested that they would be likely to notice the absence of a plan underpinning the work; they would also be likely to criticise the generic indeterminacy of this 'novel in verse', the 'anti-poetic' character of Evgenii, and the style in general. Initial, minor reviews of Chapter I, however, were favourable, despite the claim by N.A. Polevoi in his enthusiastic study in 1825 that various unimpressed critics had commented negatively on the text (these critics did not actually exist).[1] Comments continued to be positive,[2] with particular praise given to the dream sequence,[3] until the appearance of Chapter VII in *Moskovskii Vestnik* in 1827.[4] It was then felt that Pushkin had lost his way; according to Faddei Bulgarin, the chapter was most slapdash and disappointing.[5] Critics were rightly aware of a change in the work between Chapters VI and VII, between which Pushkin had dispensed with the presence of all his main characters except Tat'iana, and had ruthlessly transplanted the latter to Moscow. The 'newness' of the text, critics claimed, had also worn off (Zelinskii, III: 2-6). Chapter VIII was better received, particularly as critics began to adapt to the idea that the work should not be regarded as a complete and patterned text, but as something more 'open', a framework within which Pushkin had placed his verses.

What major issues, apart from the 'lack of plan' to which Pushkin himself had referred in his Foreword, had critics uncovered? Polevoi's 1825 remarks on the *narodnost'* of the text sparked off a polemic with D.V. Venevitinov, whose 1825 'Otvet g. Polevomu' argued for a better understanding of *narodnost'* than could be seen from Polevoi's encomium. However, a belief in the text's national feeling was reiterated by S. Shevyrev in 1841 in his discussion of the question of Pushkin's relationship to Western models. Russian critics preferred, unsurprisingly, to see their poet as no mere imitator. Not only was Pushkin the first really Russian author, whose works far surpassed the derivative novels and verse of many 18th-century authors, but he became the first Russian writer to be fashioned into an icon for each successive age. Each generation of Pushkin readers and critics has tended to 'create its own Pushkin anthology...fashioning a more homogenous image of Pushkin in accordance with its literary and ideological agenda' (Greenleaf, 1994: 5). Thus, according to their own strict ideas on the function of art, Belinskii and Gogol saw him as a national poet in the 30s and 40s, P.V. Annenkov in the 50s fashioned the image of Pushkin as a metaphysical writer, Pisarev condemned him in the 60s as socially irrelevant, Tolstoi in the 70s praised Pushkin's sense of social hierarchies, and Dostoevskii gloated over Pushkin's 'unifying' spirituality in the 80s.[6]

The first critic to devote much attention to Pushkin's *Onegin* was Vissarion Belinskii, whose articles, published in 1843-6 (eleven in all, two specifically on the novel), focussed on the characters, particularly on Onegin, whom he saw as a type of dissatisfaction and disillusionment, a suffering egoist ('stradaiushchii egoist'). The novel was Russia's first 'national-artistic work' representing the moral physiognomy of the social class to which Onegin belonged. it was also a text faithful to reality, although reality was reproduced 'artistically' (Belinskii, 1953-9, viii: 454).[7]

The appearance of the P.V. Annenkov edition of a Pushkin Collected Works in 1855 stimulated renewed interest in Pushkin's work in general, and also furthered the debate between the utilitarian critics, such as Pisarev (as well as Chernyshevskii and Dobroliubov) and the aesthetic critics, who preferred to stress Pushkin's poetic genius rather than his social directives. D.I. Pisarev's attack on Pushkin in 1865 in *Russkoe slovo,* for example, hinged on the belief that Pushkin was not socially useful.[8] To Pisarev, Onegin was no suffering soul (as Belinskii had claimed), but merely a man satiated with pleasures, and, what is worse, a hypocrite, as his attitude towards his dying uncle suggests. Onegin was, to Pisarev, a moral infant, a man with an undeveloped mind and conscience (Pisarev, 1864: 311), and not particularly representative of a social class (Pisarev reserves this literary role for Griboedov's Chatskii).

It was not Pushkin's novel itself which Pisarev particularly derided, but its reputation as a social manifesto; Pisarev thought *Onegin* rather an 'insignificant trifle' (Pisarev, 1955-6: iii, 362). Articles by aesthetic critics such as M.N. Katkov (1856) and Apollon Grigor'ev (1859) continued the debate on the novel's social relevance. However, the latter decades of the 19th century saw the creation of the Pushkin 'myth', within which all such arguments were subsumed. The myth was developed and explored throughout the Pushkin *prazdniki*, the first of which took place in 1880 (three days' worth of speeches and commemoration). Such Pushkin celebrations, which involved not only speeches and publications but the erecting of monuments to the poet, provided a focus for the ongoing debate about the rightful place of literature and its 'liberating role' (Levitt, 1989: 3). Such 'holidays' (primarily for the intelligentsia, as Levitt has noted, 1989: 15) focussed more on the topics of cultural progression and free expression than on Pushkin.

Amongst the speechmakers prominent at the 1880 *prazdnik*, Dostoevskii was to make a significant, if not altogether helpful, contribution to the critical perception of *Evgenii Onegin* in his depiction of the 'wandering' type of Onegin, who is contrasted to the 'narodnyi' (i.e. 'rooted' in the Russian soil) Tat'iana, establishing paradigmatic, if simplified views of the two main characters. Dostoevskii's penchant for broad emotional criticism had been already revealed in his hailing of Pushkin as the great national poet who combined both Western and Russian elements, knowing the 'great secret' of how to do this. Dostoevskii claimed that Pushkin had given Russia more faith in its Russianness, more confidence in its own powers; he was a prophetic poet who appeared 'at the dawning of Russia's consciousness'.[9]

Other celebrations followed, such as the fiftieth anniversary of Pushkin's death in 1887 (an anniversary surrounded by argument as to how the date was to be celebrated), and the centenary of his birth in 1899.[10] Amongst the welter of Pushkin commentary, most continued the eulogistic line and discussed the key areas established by Belinskii, to whom the novel was (a) realistic, (b) a triumph of *narodnost'* (i.e. of 'Russianness'), with Tat'iana a quintessentially Russian 'type', and (c) a socio-political work. The third of these issues has arguably been the major topic for Russian criticism of Pushkin until recently. Voskresenskii wrote in 1887 that in the novel Pushkin had provided a 'picture of Russian society, captured at one of the most interesting moments of its development' (Voskresenskii, 1887: 16), while V. Kachanovskii wrote the following year of Pushkin's holding up a mirror to society (Kachanovskii, 1888: 28). I. S. Nekrasov stated that *Onegin* provided an opportunity for social self-analysis ('poznanie samogo sebia', Nekrasov, 1887: 10).

V.O. Kliuchevskii added to this belief that Pushkin had encapsulated an ongoing social tendency when he stressed the idea of 'types' in his 1887 publication '"Onegin" i ego predki', arguing that Evgenii had 'historico-genetic ancestors' (Kliuchevskii, 1959: 409). These 'ancestors' were members of the gentry affected by 19th-century new thinking, who (apart from becoming innovators, or pessimists) partook of Onegin's mood of apathy (being at the mercy of a 'nastroenie, lisavshee ikh sposobnosti i okhoty delat' chto-nibud'', Kliuchevskii, 1959: 423). Onegin's ancestors, like his descendants, were clearly 'superfluous men' (lishnie liudi'), 'Oblomov' types, as outlined in N.A. Dobroliubov's article 'Chto takoe oblomovshchina' (1859), in which the central character of I.A. Goncharov's 1859 novel *Oblomov* is described as the embodiment of the social malaise of inertia.

In general, Pushkin criticism of the 19th century, despite some moments of perception, was painted with a broad brush in which Pushkin's genius, his status as a national poet, and his encapsulation of certain 'Russian' character traits dominant during the 1820s all merged into a confused impression of a profoundly important but yet not very well understood work.

Twentieth-century Russian criticism

Belinskii's emphasis on the realism of the work recurred in the work of critics such as D.N. Ovsianiko-Kulikovskii, R.V. Ivanov-Razumnik and N.A. Kotliarevskii. Ovsianko-Kulikovskii's chapter in *Voprosy psikhologii tvorchestva* (1902),[12] his *Istoriia russkoi intelligentsii: Itogi russkoi khudozhestvennoi literatury XIX v.* (1906, reprinted 1914), Kotliarevskii's chapter on *Onegin* in his *Literaturnye napravleniia aleksandrovskoi epokhi* (1907), and Ivanov-Razumnik's 'Evgenii Onegin' (1907) continued the Belinskiian approach of categorising Onegin and Tat'iana as 'types' such as the 'superfluous' man, or the strong Russian maiden. Stating that Pushkin was never a Romantic, Ivanov-Razumnik discussed Pushkin's optimistic subjectivity, which contradicts the romantic gloom commonly found in Romantic heroes. The significance of the subjective element, which counterbalances the so-called realism, or objectivity of the text, was a topic introduced hesitantly by both Ovsianko-Kulikovskii and Kotliarevskii, who suggested that the work contains a lyrical author, who interweaves a poet's confession into an objective work. However, the conclusion reached was that the work, despite its lyricism, 'must be regarded as a work of predominately objective art' (Ovsianko-Kulikovskii, 1914: 86). The realist bias towards the work, despite such hints as the above regarding the subjective element, was to continue until the twenties, when it encountered its first real opposition, and on into the sixties.[13]

1910 was the year in which B.L. Modzalevskii's catalogue of Pushkin's library appeared;[14] more notoriously, it was the year in which P.O. Morozov announced the discovery of fragments of the so-called 'Tenth Chapter', thought to have been destroyed. This find has given rise to an entire sub-school of argument (see pp. 20-22 for a brief discussion of the Tenth Chapter), although, given the unfinished nature of these fragments, this critical line can only be of limited value. It did serve to perpetuate interest in the political aspect of the work, a theme in which Soviet critics naturally showed a great deal of interest. N.L. Brodskii's 1932 commentary, for example, although a useful addendum to the novel,[15] has some rather simplistic socialist points relating to Pushkin's satire against the Russian aristocracy. Dmitrii Blagoi has followed a similar line, adopting a sociological approach, writing in 1929 of Pushkin's concern with class identity and his view of Russian society (although Blagoi's view of a possible way forward for the nobility was later criticised by Soviet scholars).

The revolution called into question the entire status of literature, its relevance to an emerging new state and consciousness. The critic Boris Eikhenbaum in 1921 called for a fundamental rethinking of Pushkin's place in Russian culture, a new and more relevant way of approaching his texts that would not be as 'schoolboyish' as he believed past criticism of the novel to have been.[16] One method of rethinking was somewhat drastic; to those iconoclastic writers and critics who belonged to the – at times – rather aggressively political Futurist movement (1911-30), Pushkin was someone, who, as Maiakovskii suggested in his play *Misteriia-Buff* (1918), should be 'thrown out' along with other outdated cultural artefacts. If Pushkin was not to be ejected, then some use had to be found for him, presumably in terms of the lessons he might have to offer for ideologues. Such a lesson was established in 1934. This was an important year for Russian literature as a whole, being the time of the adoption of the official literary doctrine of socialist realism and consequent stress on the social responsibility of the author, his ideological correctness, and his realism. It was in this year that a three-volume edition devoted to Pushkin appeared in the *Literaturnoe nasledstvo* series; it contained primary material as well as criticism by scholars such as Boris Tomashevskii (on the 10th chapter) and Ivan Vinogradov, amongst others. The line uniformly underpinning these articles is the realist one; Pushkin's ideology is the focus. A shift in his ideological position, revealed in the way the characters change, i.e. Tat'iana from a girl to the epitome of the Russian soul, is noted, particularly by Vinogradov; yet Pushkin is, ultimately, seen as a writer who capitulated to the regime.

The year following the 3-volume edition, 1935, saw the structures agreed for the creation of an All-Union Pushkin Committee; Pushkin was officially a 'great Russian poet' as well as being the father of Russian literature, and the 'creator of the Russian language'. Clearly, this 'capitulator' would have to be seen in a more positive light, and subsequent Soviet criticism therefore stressed the poet's revolutionary ideals, his 'nationalism', and, once again, his realism. Asking in 1936 what Pushkin 'gives the proletarian reader', Maksim Gor'kii answered that the essence lay in the author's analysis of his social milieu: 'he objectively describes for us this (social) class...as an unsuccessful and disorganised part of historical experience' (Gor'kii, 1953, 562). *Onegin* was treated very much in the Belinskiian manner, in terms of its content, the 'mirror' it held up to reality (Pushkin was hailed as the 'first Russian realist' by Konstantin Simonov at the celebration of 150 years since Pushkin's birth in 1949),[18] and its value-system. The 1937 Pushkin Centennial established the 'Pushkin Year', with publications, activities and ceremonies designed to bring the great 'father of literature' to all people throughout the USSR. Farms, factories, etc., were named for the poet, whose iconoclasm had been submerged in the hysteria of patriotic feeling for this 'national genius'; Pushkin became a 'quasi-divinity' (Levitt, 1989: 166). It is arguably significant that the year of such polishing of Pushkin's image, 1937, was also a good year for show trials and purges directed against the pre-revolutionary intelligentsia; Pushkin was possibly held up as an example of the positive *intelligent* (Levitt, 1989: 163-6).

If Pushkin was now a positive 'new man', then his best-known hero must also be so. Critics such as Blagoi in 1931 and 1955, B.S. Meilakh in 1949, G.A. Gukovskii in 1957, G.P. Makogonenko in 1957 and 1963, Boris Tomashevskii in 1961 and S. Bondi in 1978 concentrated on the concept of Onegin as a 'positive hero' (a prerogative for a socialist realist work), analysing his 'scepticism' (rather an interesting euphemism for his 'khandra') as a natural outcome of social events (Meilakh, 1949: 106), and looking also at Pushkin's Decembrist leanings, his realism, and on the national ideas implicit in the work. The next great jubilee, in 1949, added a new patriotic emphasis to Pushkin in these post-war years while re-emphasising his realism. Every household now had a copy of this supposedly model writer with his model messages.

This concentration on content and 'message' was only partly counteracted by studies of Pushkin's style and language by Tomashevskii (1918), V. Vinogradov (1935 and 1941)[19] and G. O. Vinokur (1941). Tomashevskii's study of Pushkin's iambic line in *Onegin* offered a workmanlike analysis of the poetics of the novel, and was furthered by Vinokur, who, writing on the organisation of the stanzas, and the shift of themes from stanza to stanza, offered a valuable alternative to the simplistic, sociological view of the structure. Vinokur analysed the effect on stanzaic organisation of language, developing a line suggested by Tynianov in 1924 on the effect of structure on semantics.

A stronger reaction, inevitably, to the dominant 'realist' reading of the text had to occur, and such a reaction can be traced to the 1920s in Russia and the work of the Formalist critics, to whom the text is of interest according to its devices and techniques. The post-Belinskiian realist approach was firmly denied (although unfortunately, not defeated) by the two best-known Formalist critics, Viktor Shklovskii and Iurii Tynianov. Radically departing from the old realist approach, Shklovskii in 1923 compared *Onegin* with Laurence Sterne's digressive novel *Tristram Shandy* (1759-67), concluding that the text is a parody à la Sterne, and argued that the real plot was not the story, but the manipulation of devices:

> The true plot of 'Evgenii Onegin' is not the story of Onegin and Tat'iana, but the game (played) with this story. The main content of the novel is its own constructive forms ('sobstvennye konstruktivnye formy'); the plot form is used as real objects are used in the pictures of Picasso. (Shklovskii, 1923, 'Evgenii Onegin: Pushkin i Stern': 211)

Also following the Formalist approach, Iu. N. Tynianov in 1921-2 wrote on the composition of the work ('O kompozitsii Evgeniia Onegina', published only in 1974, again in 1975 and 1977), with the intent of defining the difference between poetry and prose. Tynianov saw an inherent literariness and tension in the text, two key ideas deriving from Pushkin's intent to combine a 'plan for a lofty novel' ('plan *vysokogo* romana') with a plan for a novel about everyday life' ('s planom romana bytogo', Tynianov, 1977: 67), and described the work as a novel about a novel/romance (a 'roman romana', punning on the two meanings of the word 'roman'; Tynianov, 1977: 58). Arguing that the structure of the novel rests not on plot but on verbal composition, or the verbal dynamics of the work, he sees the text as a work in which the verse 'deforms' the novelistic construction, creating something quite new:

> The deformation of the novel by verse was expressed in the deformation of both small units and large – and ultimately, the entire novel appears conclusively deformed: from the merging of two elements, from their mutual battle and mutual interpenetration a new form was born. (Tynianov, 1977: 75)

In the work of Tynianov and Shklovskii a radically new approach had been offered, intended to counteract the critics' insistence on the didactic message or socio-nationalistic points to be found in the novel. However, Formalist criticism was mistrusted and even unpublishable in the new post-revolutionary era. Even the work of Mikhail Bakhtin on the nature of the digressive author (1940; published 1965, reprinted 1975) had no effect on the literary critical establishment.[20] Bakhtin discusses the development of linguistic consciousness, in terms of the interweaving of the authorial 'prosaic' voice with, for example, Lenskii's poetic tones, which are separated from the prose voice through parodic intonation (Bakhtin, 1975: 411). Arguing that there is no 'direct Pushkinian word' in the text, or any linguistic centre to the work, Bakhtin argued that the author is located at the centre of 'intersecting dimensions' ('nakhoditsia v organizatsionnom tsentre peresecheniia ploskostei', Bakhtin, 1975: 415). Perhaps surprisingly, Bakhtin did not go on to discuss the text in terms of his concept of carnival, which sees the text as constantly exploding and imploding any closed meanings into textual openness, permitting many different interpretations.

The approach offered by the Formalists had to be developed outside of the then Soviet Union; Roman Jakobson wrote briefly on the dominance of the verse plane in the work, arguing that consequently the characters are not 'real' (1937, published only in 1975). Jakobson suggested that Pushkin has created what he terms 'oscillating characterisations', or contradictory characters unsusceptible to exegesis; indeed, the entire novel is so 'elastically polysemantic' that it cannot be explained by any single idea (Jakobson, 1975: 55, 54).

The jubilee years of 1962 (the 125th anniversary of Pushkin's death) and 1974 (the 175th anniversary of his birth) continued the eulogistic line. In 1962 the number of volumes of Pushkin published in Russian topped eighty-seven million; Pushkin was everywhere, in films, plays, in magazines, newspapers, journals, even political speeches (Levitt, 1989: 168-9). However, in the 1960s the development of structuralist ideas of literary criticism offered a chance to develop the Soviet line, and to incorporate several of the ideas offered by the Formalists, much of whose work was only published in the 60s and 70s. The chief proponent of this critical school in Russia, Iurii Lotman, produced a valuable article, 'Khudozhestvennaia struktura Evgeniia Onegina', in 1966. Lotman looked at Onegin as the 'embryo' of the subsequent history of the Russian novel, but also defined neatly the 'inverted system' of the novel, in terms of which Pushkin exposes the falsity of a romantically idealistic model of the world. Lotman developed Tynianov's idea that the tension in the work derives chiefly from the interplay of two stylistic systems (poetry and prose, or the 'lofty novel' and the 'novel about everyday life'), a tension giving rise to the irony so clearly to be noted in *Onegin*. However, Lotman ultimately moves back towards a realist interpretation in the collection of articles/lectures which appeared in 1975 (*Roman v stikhakh Pushkina 'Evgenii Onegin'*), in his attempt to fuse a formalist concentration on the devices of the text with an analysis of its ideological 'realism'.[21]

Lotman's ideas, centred on the concept of 'point of view', show not only a debt to the Formalists but to Bakhtin, whose concept of polyphony makes an appearance in Lotman's discussion on 'non-authorial' voices which allows the text to be read both 'authorially and 'non-authorially'; the novel is dialogic, or even polylogic ('ili dazhe polilogichen', Lotman, 1975: 87). Lotman uncovers a fundamental paradox, that *Onegin* can be interpreted as written either in 'authorial monologue', or in multiple narrative voices ('mnogogolosie'); either approach is equally correct (Lotman, 1975: 87). Primarily, Lotman brought to the fore the principle of structural opposition so seminal to the work; in particular, he emphasised the notion that the world depicted in the text is constructed according to a contrast between 'reality' and the artificial viewpoint encouraged by the allusions. This constructive principle, one which opens up the full complexity of the text, and frustrates any conclusive reading, has become the primary concern for other scholars and in particular for S.G. Bocharov, who produced the most sophisticated of Soviet analyses of the work in 1974.[23] Other work in the 70s focussed on Pushkin's work in general, and offered overviews of the text, such as Lakshin's article on Pushkin's own evolution during the time of writing, or concentrated on rather limited aspects of *Onegin*, such as Turbin's curious article on the similarities between the *Onegin* stanza and the Cathedral of our Saviour.[25]

Bocharov follows the phenomenological line[26] in his analysis of the way in which consciousness is represented in the text, and suggests an inherent dualism to be found in the structure of depicted awareness. Discussing the Tynianov/Bakhtin/Lotman polyphonic approach, Bocharov labels the device of using various stylistic ways of reporting on events 'heterostylism'.[27] Suggesting that the novel is 'gnoseological', i.e. that the search for knowledge (which appears shrouded in mystery), is the main concern, Bocharov defines textual reality as sited at the intersecting planes of subjectivity and objectivity. Bocharov's ideas are crystallised in the words 'translations and switchovers' ('perevody i perekliucheniia', Bocharov, 1974: 70-1) which he uses to describe transitions from one stylistic language to another, i.e. from one reality to another. The characters are 'distorted' due to the influence of foreign literature; they search for a style, for reality, like the reader, who is also manipulated towards gnoseological engagement.

Bocharov's work remains the most exciting Russian criticism on the text, despite the post-*glasnost'* (i.e. post-1986) emphasis not only on rehabilitating hitherto unpublishable authors but also on re-evaluating the great classics and the themes and ideas so lauded in them. The shift towards a new Soviet and Russian 'pan-human alternative thinking' (Mondry, 1990: 32), in terms of which not *narodnost'*, for example, but 'universality' and 'humanism' in classical literature were to be lauded, was apparent even in 1986 at the Pushkin House conference,[28] and has had some consequences for Pushkin criticism since. Pushkin, as the great god of realism and Sovietised thinking, remains the major figure for re-analysis – although whether of the kind suggested by Mikhail Amlinskii, who has allegedly discovered Pushkin's secret diary from 1836-7, an erotic account of the author's lovelife, is somewhat debatable.[29] As Gorovskii wrote in 1987, a campaign dedicated to rehabilitating Pushkin is an essentially spiritual task (Gorovskii, 1987: 5); possibly one which offers hope for the reanimation of Russian culture in a broader (and vaguer) sense. 'Pushkinology' is, after all, 'Russianology' (Zalygin, 1987: 4). Pushkin is the most holy of holies (Levitt, 1989: 174); in a Russian literary environment which seems convulsed with self-disgust, and which now produces literature of the most grimly real, or grotesque kind, a literature filled with images of guilt and impotence in reaction to the tainted legacy of the Stalinist past, the fate of such 'holiness' will prove to be a useful way of measuring cultural self-appraisal.

In terms of specific work on *Evgenii Onegin*, there is still a need for a major new study; although the sesquicentennial of Pushkin's death in 1987 saw many new works appearing, these were largely of a biographical and celebratory nature. Among recent work on the novel itself, there have been articles focussing on limited aspects, such as Murav'eva's on (amongst other topics), the treatment of silence in the work (1987),[30] Turbin's on links with Pushkin's *Boris Godunov* (1987),[31] Baevskii's work on repetitions (1989),[32] Iskrin's on Tat'iana's dream (1989),[33] Solov'eva's and Barlas's linguistic articles on comparisons, syntax, rhetoric and 'expressivity' (1989),[34] Mikhailova's article on the 'oratorical' nature of the text (1989),[35] or Bocharov's article on the French epigraph to the novel (from a paper given at the Paris conference in 1987, published only in 1991).[36] Baevskii's 1990 critical study of the text is rather limited, appearing to have grown out of discussions with students on certain words and phrases (i.e. he discusses Chapter I, stanza 23, a verse containing references to trade with England), and on topics such as memory and alienation.[37]

Articles in the nineties have included V. Matsapura's look at some 19th-century Ukrainian imitations of the novel (1990),[38] Iurii Nishikov's look at the character of Evgenii in the context of historicism (1991),[39] Makhov's comparison of the metaphor of the magic crystal with the 19th-century writer Nikolai Konshin's similar image in his *Vladitel' volshebnogo khrustal'ka* (1991),[40] N. Khardzhiev's and M. Iskrin's very brief analyses of certain phrases in the text (1990-91),[41] S. Freilikh's analysis of both Pushkin's and the film-maker Eizenshtein's use of parody (1991),[42] S. Fomichev's argument that sources for the novel can be found in the work of Pushkin's contemporary, Küchelbecker (1992),[43] while Iurii Lotman touched on the ideas of death and possibility in the text in his musings on Hegelian concepts of realised unrealisability (1992),[44] and V. Turbin offered a rather whimsical look at the text's epic qualities and social significance (1993).[45]

Papers at the second International Pushkin Conference (26 May – 1 June, Tver', 1993) included a look at the English words and terms in the novel (V.S. Baevskii) and a discussion on translating the text (papers by J. van Baak and S. Mitchell). At this conference, N.I. Mikhailova outlined a project aimed at the creation of an '*Onegin* encyclopaedia' which would include a dictionary of personal and mythological names, an explanatory dictionary, and a dictionary of motifs, as well as other appendices.[46] The same N.I. Mikhailova's rather disappointingly fragmented 1994 study (with illustrations) of *Onegin* contains two useful dictionary appendices on vocabulary and names in the work, and is devoted to a discussion of key terms in the text and to the 'atmosphere' surrounding Pushkin as he wrote each section of the work.

There is still place for a new, deeper look – alongside the development of a new cultural awareness of Russia herself – at this seminal text which has so long been hailed as the essence of 'Russianness'; but until Pushkin himself has ceased to be synonymous with 'Culture', Pushkin studies may continue to be mere idolatry. The 200th anniversary of Pushkin's birth to be held in 1999 may herald a new era, but given the current crisis in Russian scholarship, suffering from lack of resources, manpower, and direction, it is doubtful whether Pushkin's homeland will produce the definitive new edition of the author's works in time.

Western criticism

Cizevsky's translation and commentary appeared in 1953, with an 'introduction' in which he has one good, albeit brief point to remind the reader of, namely, the mock-epic nature of the verse; he also includes comment on the *Onegin* stanza, (1953: x-xiv), a topic discussed by Scherr (1986: 237-6), and by Nabokov (1964: 9-14). Prior to his critical commentary there had been little for the Western scholar to read in English; although D.S. Mirskii's comments had been available in English since 1926 in his four-times reprinted edition, they provided only five fairly general pages on the novel (pp. 87-92). Edmund Wilson's 1936 essay, written for the centenary of Pushkin's death in 1937 for a non-specialist audience, concentrated on retelling the plot, and on suggesting a cultural framework within which the text might be appreciated.[47] Arguing for Pushkin's Keatsian skill at nature depiction, he concludes that the texts most comparable to it are Stendhal's *Le Rouge et le Noir* and *Flaubert's Madame Bovary*. Janko Lavrin's chapter on the text in his *Pushkin and Russian Literature* (1947) offers another overview of the plot, while arguing that the text is the medium for Pushkin's 'double verdict on romanticism', and demonstrates his philosophy of 'acceptance of life' (Lavrin, 1947: 139), two ideas which have reappeared in many other critical studies of the work. Until the 60s no in-depth English-language analysis of the work had appeared, apart from Ralph Matlaw's 1959 analysis of Tat'iana's dream, a subject of ongoing interest to many scholars (see the section below).[48]

The text was made much more accessible to a wider readership in the sixties, with the appearance in 1963-4 of three English translations, but the majority of critical comments remained brief. Henry Gifford's overview of the Russian novel (1964) gave the work only five pages which focus on the question of its status as a 'novel'. F.D. Reeve's thirty-page overview in 1966 promoted the idea that the tension in the novel derives from the difference 'between the real and the artificial, between the original and the imitation, between the poet as hero and the banalities of everyday life' (Reeve, 1966: 17). He defines *Onegin* as 'an attempt to create a literary genre, the socially apt realistic novel in the nineteenth century' (Reeve, 1966: 39), a statement which he later qualifies by arguing that the essence of the work is the 'struggle by an individual against his socially determined limitations' (Reeve, 1966: 44). More specific studies also appeared during the 60s, such as Richard Gustafson's 1962 discussion of the metaphor of the seasons, in which he draws attention to Pushkin's 'philosophical' concern with the passage of time (Gustafson, 1962: 7) as indicated by the movement in the work from spring, season of youth, joy and love, to winter, season of loss and disappointment. Another article appeared on Tat'iana's dream (Nesaule, 1968), while Stanley Mitchell, writing on Tat'iana's reading in 1968, examined the links between the novels *Clarissa*, *Julie* and *Delphine* in order to point out the differences between Pushkin's heroine and her fictional heroines.

Only in the 70s did *Onegin* begin to receive more sophisticated treatment, although general overviews still appeared, such as A.F. Boyd's 1972 chapter devoted on the cultural background to the world, and Onegin as a 'superfluous man' and as a 'Russian dandy'. In 1970 Walter Vickery entered the critical arena with a twenty-seven-page assessment of the text in which, amongst many sensible comments, he argued that although the novel is about love and Romanticism, it is primarily about death, which 'allows of no salvaging, no healing' (Vickery, 1970: 111). Pointing to the fact of Lenskii's death (which critics often omit from their summaries, and even discussion, of the text), he noted, briefly, that from the novel the reader understands how life offers no second chances; once Lenskii is dead, he remains so, while Onegin fails to win Tat'iana. Time is irrevocably lost, suggests Vickery, arguing that this seemingly light and airy novel is filled with a deep sorrow at the 'thought of no return' (Vickery, 1970, 129).

The year after Vickery's work, as well as articles dealing with intertextuality (a comparison with Nabokov's *Ada*, Johnson, 1971), and with the tone of the text (McLean, 1971), John Bayley's *Pushkin: A Comparative Commentary* appeared. As its title suggests, it offers some illuminating views on Pushkin's place in European literature. Taking up Shklovskii's point, that the novel is, like *Tristram Shandy*, a text which focusses attention on form rather than content, Bayley defines it as a text of sentiment.[49] In his forty-seven-page analysis he examines the 'delicate balance of parody and sentiment' (Bayley, 1971: 248) as he takes the reader through the main stylistic and thematic strands interwoven in the novel. The comparative line continued in Irwin Weil's 1974 study of links between the text and the poet Malfilâtre, and in Hoisington's 1975 article on the text as an 'inverted Byronic poem'. 1975 was also the year of a minor debate in the *New Zealand Slavonic Journal*; V. Dvinin, responding to T.E. Little's analysis of the parodic features of the work, in terms of which Onegin is a Byronic hero, and Tat'iana a sentimental heroine, protested at the conclusion that the work is ironic. Dvinin's points are somewhat undermined by his claim that 'only a Russian can understand Tatyana' (1975: 86). A useful study of irony appeared the following year, with Sona Hoisington's published paper on the 'hierarchy of narratees' in the work, and on the responses elicited from the implied reader of Onegin through the use of irony:

> The victims of the irony...are the two mock audiences: Poet-Friends and Reader. Each of these mock audiences is identified with one of the work's central characters: Poet-friends with fellow poet Lenskii and Reader with that contemporary fellow Petersburgite, Onegin. (Hoisington, 1976: 249)

Bayley's book is directly echoed in Richard Freeborn's study, published two years later, in which the author builds on Bayley's comment on the 'paradox of regularity and changeability' to be found in the *Onegin* stanza (Freeborn, 1973: 12). Also in 1973, J. Fennell examined the style of the work, and, continuing the dualistic line adopted by critics aware of the prose/poetry dichotomy in the text, offered a useful definition of the 'prosaic' style and suggested that the work is a 'monument to poetic craftsmanship', an expression of the author's development from a youthful poetic mode to a mature prose style (Fennell: 1973: 55). This critical focus on the struggle between prose and poetry in the text, the consensus being that prose 'wins', is also to be found in *Onegin* criticism of the 1980s, such as James Woodward's 1982 article on the 'principle of contradictions' in the novel. Developing Lotman's view that certain contradictory statements which appear in the text may in fact be part of the author's overall plan, he argues for the unification of all contradictions within the central theme of 'the novel of the characters' (i.e. the story), which provides a standpoint 'from which all the narrator's contradictory statements...in the work may be seen to be consistently intelligible' (Woodward, 1982: 30). Woodward's attempt to unite contradictions, such as Tat'iana's changeable attitude to love, is made through the argument that all paradoxes disappear within the 'wider context' of the characters' (i.e. Tat'iana's) resigned acceptance of life and its duties. W.M. Todd (1975, republished, 1986), takes a different view of the idea of 'duty'; he discusses the cultural range of the work and analyses 'cultural determinism', within which the characters do, however, have 'possibilities for autonomy' (Todd, 1986, 122).

Also writing on Tat'iana, Richard Gregg argued in 1981 against the 'hagiographic' interpretation of her character, preferring, as do several other critics (see Makogonenko, Briggs and Nabokov), to see her as a realistic character who combines good and bad points. Tat'iana is described by Gregg as a complex, 'broad' character who is basically resilient, and who shows a praiseworthy but practical ability to come to 'terms with a life she had not chosen' (Gregg, 1981: 11). Michael Katz also followed this line in his 1984 study of 'love and marriage' in the novel, in which he concentrates on Tat'iana's rejection of Onegin and love when she chooses duty at the end of the work.

Analysing the European 'models' for her decision (looking at the fate of Richardson's heroines, or Rousseau's Julie), Katz implies that Tat'iana, ultimately following in her mother's footsteps in resigning herself to married life with a husband she does not love, is forever bound to imitation rather than originality.

J.T. Shaw offered another viewpoint on the prose/poetry battle, suggesting in an article in 1981 that the author-persona experiences three different stages, moving from a time 'of youthful perceptivity and enchantment, followed by a stage of disenchantment, followed by a third stage (the implied present tense of narrating the novel) or mature re-enchantment' (Shaw, 1981: 30). Donald Fanger's chapter in 1983 on *Onegin* argues that the text 'must be read at the same time as a fiction and as a meditation on the writing of fiction, its expressive possibilities and limits (Fanger, 1983: 33). It is, as Clayton was later to argue, 'poetic' (Fanger, 1983: 36), and metafictional (a text about its own writing, Fanger, 1983: 40).[50] Attempting a newer approach, Roberta Clipper-Sethi argued rather unconvincingly in 1983 that the work is inherently 'dramatic', and that Pushkin was particularly influenced by contemporary Russian comedy. An interesting, if not particularly seminal viewpoint, was advanced by D.Z. Crookes in his 1984 study of the musical instruments referred to in the work (lyres, trumpets, violins, bassoon and flute and horns). Simon Franklin, writing on *Onegin* and Gogol's *Mertvye dushi* in 1984, argued that the 'unfinished' nature of *Onegin*, a problem which has occupied the attention of several critics, is a problem created 'quite deliberately' by Pushkin (Franklin, 1984: 375). Pushkin 'pretended' to leave the text unfinished, thus creating 'the illusion of possible continuation, of an open-ended life' (Franklin, 1984: 375). Thus Pushkin renders 'open' what is in fact a 'closed' text.

The eighties in Pushkin criticism were dominated by two critics: J.D. Clayton, and Sona Stephan Hoisington, who, after four articles in the 1970s and 80s, on critical responses, allusions (Byron and *Adolphe*), narration, and parody, published a useful overview of critical approaches to the work. Clayton's 1985 book, *Ice and Flame*, was the major publication of the decade and is one of only two book-length studies on the novel in English to date (the other being Briggs' 1992 study).

Clayton has published eight articles in addition to *Ice and Flame*, beginning with a 1971 study of the epigraph to *Onegin*, followed by a 1975 look at the Shakespearean allusions, a 1979 analysis of the internal chronology of the work, a discussion of Soviet critical responses to the novel, and a study of the Faustian theme, both in 1980. In 1981 an article on the symbolism of time and space in the novel appeared, offering another insight into the dominant ideas of poetic youth (associated with a longing for exotic climes) and prosaic maturity (Clayton, 1981: 56). Clayton's thesis in *Ice and Flame* is that *Onegin* is definable according to its 'lyrical kernel' (Clayton, 1985: 179), which he discusses in various ways. The lyrical essence of the work is not only expressed through the poetical nature of the text but through theme, for the novel is about the meaning and significance of poetry, in terms of the 'value' it brings to life, and the chances it offers for characters to attain freedom and inner harmony. Clayton's text is useful particularly in its overview of critical literature, its review of themes (see his 7th chapter, on the meaning of the work), and for an excellent chapter dealing with the character of Onegin.

Since 1985, Clayton has written on two other aspects of the work. His 'towards a feminist reading' (1987) developed an idea only barely hinted at previously by Gregg (1969), when he points to the overwhelming 'male sexuality' of the banquet scene in the dream sequence. Discussing Pushkin's female characters as written in either the form of the 'meek Mary' or the 'Circe' type, Helen, Clayton defines Tat'iana as an amalgam of both, split into two at the end, when the author shows his preference for the faithful Mary over the emotional Helen. The rejection of Onegin by Tat'iana expresses therefore Pushkin's desire to 'believe in the possibility of female constancy in marriage' (Clayton, 1987: 260) – a point, however, made earlier by Mirskii. Continuing Gregg's Freudian analysis (surprisingly, he does not mention Gregg's article), Clayton discusses the duel as a parallel to the defloration of woman, and suggests that in Tat'iana's dream there is a description of the heroine masturbating.

Clayton followed this article in 1988 by an analysis of the problem of plot in the novel, arguing that the problem of establishing the fabula 'manifests itself as a metaphor for the problem of destiny in the text'. Clayton hints at a less schematic reading of the text than any yet offered, in a manner reminiscent of previous claims, from Pisarev's disbelief in Pushkin as a great thinker to Bayley's likening of Pushkin to the unserious image of 'champagne'. *Evgenii Onegin* may be a text of whimsy and chance:

> Perhaps the events of life are preordained by fate (providence, god), but perhaps life is simply a game of chance...In the novel *Evgenii Onegin* the indeterminateness of the story ('neopredelennost' fabuly') is reflected in the indeterminateness of life itself, from which we create the story which we call fate.[51]

Clayton's lead has not been taken up, however: most critics are still attempting to reduce the novel to categories, sections, ideas of closure, which may be contrary to the spirit of the work. R. Gregg's 1994 analysis of stanza and plot argued that, although Evgenii himself may be a man 'at loose ends', the plot itself is distinguished by its closure (the appendages are therefore not integral to the work). It has been suggested that there is some form of resolution of paradoxes such as Shaw's third stage of 'mature re-enchantment', or the stage of 'acceptance' discussed by Vickery, Fennell, Woodward and

Gustafson). Other critics have skirted the issue of a 'theory of everything' which would define the text, concentrating on more limited aspects of the novel, such as Thomas Barran's analysis of the relationship of the narrator to Lenskii (1987),[52] or Melchior Wolff's analysis of the word 'dream' ('mechta') in the novel, used as the basis for a discussion of the anti-Romantic elements of the work.[53] In terms of publications arising from the 1987 sesquicentennial conferences, David Bethea's edition (1993) suggested the ways in which American Pushkin studies have developed (and are developing). Analyses of the text ranged from a study of dance themes (W.M. Todd) to a discussion of antenantiosis (W.E. Harkins, arguing that the term litotes, used to refer to Pushkin's negative assertions, could be replaced by this critical label),[54] to the relevance of Pushkin's African ancestry (J.T. Shaw), to an analysis of the internal dynamic of the work by L.O'Bell, who distinguishes four central elements – 'first, the demon, second, the man of the world, third, the journey, and fourth, the farewell and homecoming' (Bethea, 1993, 153). De Haard's paper from the Amsterdam sesquicentennial argued for the I-narrator as the unifying factor of the work.

The 90s in the West have also seen the publication of A.D.P. Briggs' study of the work in the *Landmarks of World Literature* series (1992), a major analysis of the text in English which is particularly useful for undergraduates (being written in a most accessible style). Briggs draws the reader's attention to the often-neglected duel scene, arguing that interpretations of the novel have ignored this event, and have, therefore, also ignored the fact of Onegin's guilt for killing Lenskii. Apart from this major study, there have been several articles, such as Priscilla Roosevelt's brief discussion of the 'contrasting responses to nature' shown by the characters,[55] Ryan and Wigzell's 1992 analysis of the *Svetlana* link,[56]and Levitt's 1993 semiotic study.[57] More comparative studies are likely following Richard Tempest's comparison of aspects of *Pride and Prejudice* with *Onegin*,[58] J. Garrard's reappraisal of the Byronic motif,[59] and T. Miller's thoughts on the influence of Pushkin's novel on two texts by Lermontov.[60] Emerson's reappraisal of Tati'iana provides one of the better analyses of the contradictions inherent in this character;[61] Nancy Downey's dissertation on the theme of memory in the novel, if published, should provide information on another interesting aspect.[62]

Can *Evgenii Onegin* ever be defined satisfactorily in terms of its intent, message, genre or significance? A general 'theory of everything' must recognise the tensions inherent in the work, which strain against any closure, and which create shifting patterns. Jan Meijer discussed the way in which the text defines yet outgrows its own forms and must go beyond itself (Meijer, 1968: 143). Any critical 'boundary' which can be placed around the work is one which can always be crossed, for *Onegin* is an essentially liminal and ludic work in which Pushkin plays with the rules of the game.

The rules are acknowledged, but the players constantly try and cross them, as does the author himself. Monika Greenleaf is correct in her statement that the text is one that 'fights the reader's tendency to seek closure' (Greenleaf, 1994: 17).[63]

Greenleaf argues that *Onegin* as a 'deliberately fabricated Romantic fragment poem' (Greenleaf, 1994: 206) in which the reader can never achieve a stable perspective, but only exercises his evaluative faculty. The best approaches to the novel, in this author's view, remain those in which the critic understands the text's focus on issues such as subjectivity and fragmentation. Helena Goscilo has developed the line outlined by Bocharov in her study of Pushkin's 'concern with epistemology and representation' in the work (1990: 271). The text is, as Bocharov (in his study of the gnoseological concept embedded in the text) suggested, is an epistemological exercise which cannot be completed but in which the process itself is the focus. Bocharov has argued for a shifting mutability in the work, in terms of which the style constantly changes, describing a gnoseological process. M.C. Levitt's semiotic study (1993) suggested that the unity of *Onegin* rests in a dynamic concept, which he defines as existing at several levels centred on the theme of 'identity versus role' (a topic it would have been useful to have developed), or, as he expresses it, 'an equation, an often shifting dialectical relationship, as a problem of maintaining distance between aspects of self, or, in semiotic terms, between signifier and signified' (Levitt, 1993: 445).

Work remains to be done in the sphere of semiotics (developing Levitt's ideas), feminist critical theory, deconstruction, and reader-response theory; scholarship on *Onegin* will undoubtedly prove to be a fruitful field of research for many decades yet.

One of the critical approaches to the work as yet undeveloped is the Bakhtinian carnival approach, which defines a text as 'open' and ambivalent, filled with structures that are overturned. The obvious question is, why did Bakhtin himself not define the work as a carnival text? He had, after all, suggested the genre definition of another Pushkin text, the story 'Pikovaia dama', as a Menippean satire, which in Bakhtin's definition is a 'weakened' form of carnival text. Despite Bakhtin's concentration on polyphony in *Evgenii Onegin* rather than carnival, a case can be made for a carnivalist reading of the novel. If this definition is premised, then *Onegin* can be examined as a seriocomic, innovative genre in which the main intent, as in all carnival texts, is to reveal truths through explosive laughter.

Key issues

Certain features of the novel have occasioned particular sub-schools of criticism. There are flourishing schools of scholarship concerned, for example, with allusions in the work, and with the definition of the two main protagonists' characters, issues which will be addressed in Part III. Two very specific areas of scholarship have grown up around the question of the significance and placing of the 10th chapter, and around the crucial scene of Tat′iana's dream.

The 'Tenth Chapter'

Since Pavel Morozov's sensational announcement in 1910 of the existence of 'coded' verses by Pushkin, all that remain of a destroyed tenth chapter, critics have been debating the authenticity, the meaning, extent and ordering of these fragments.[64]

About the linkage between the verses found by Morozov and *Onegin* there is still some doubt. The proof that a tenth chapter did exist rests on several points: (1) that a manuscript of the 10th chapter was in fact given to Nicholas I to read, as attested to by A.O. Smirnova-Rosset; (2) that Pushkin wrote in the margin of the manuscript of his story 'Metel′' on October 20, 1830, that he had burned the 10th Canto the day before; (3) there is also a note in the margin of 'Onegin's journey' referring to the 10th chapter; and (4) a note in the margin of the *Notebooks;* (5) there is also the remark made to Mikhail Iuzefovich by Pushkin, in which he stated that he had intended Onegin to become a Decembrist – the fragments deal with the Decembrist movement. More positive proof comes from (6) notes from Pushkin's contemporaries such as A. A. Kononov, and, in particular, a note in Viazemskii's diary, in which he recalls Pushkin reciting several of the stanzas from the chapter; and (7) a letter from Aleksandr Turgenev to his brother in which he quotes from *Onegin* stanzas dealing with the Decembrist uprising, which appear in the fragments found by Morozov.[65]

What do these fragments contain? They have not been completely deciphered, but there is agreement on the following general content. These verses described briefly below refer to the version given in the BCP edition of *Evgenii Onegin.*

1 – this stanza refers to Aleksandr I, a 'ruler weak and wily'.

2 – and to his impotence during the Napoleonic campaign and probably to the defeat at Austerlitz;

3 – reiterates this theme;

4 & 5 – continue in this anti-tsarist vein.

6 & 7 – contain hypothetical ideas on what the tsar could do for Russia; the word 'avos', or 'perchance', is used as a 'shibboleth' of the Russian people, i.e. a distinguishing word which reveals a fundamental aspect of their national identity.

8 – refers to Napoleon.

9 – depicts the political situation in Europe – uprisings in Spain, Naples

and Greece. This stanza also contains one indecipherable line (Nabokov omits it, I, 316; see Cizevsky, pp 311-312 for some possible ways of translating the encoded message).

10 – refers to the 'Aleksandrovskii kholop', i.e. the 'slave of Aleksandr', with probable reference to General Aleksis Arakcheev, Aleksandr I's Prime Minister (although Nabokov appears to believe it refers simply to the rule of law becoming the 'despot's slave', III: 333).

11 – the revolt which took place in 1821 in the ranks of the Semenovskii regiment is alluded to.

12-15 – refer to the development of the Decembrist movement, which met at 'Nikita's' (Nikita Murave′v's, in St Petersburg), and at 'Il′ia's' (Il′ia Dolgorukii's house). Pushkin refers also to the Decembrists Mikhail Lunin, Ivan Iakushkin and Nikolai Turgenev (the lines on the latter being the subject of Turgenev's letter to his brother, see above); he also refers to himself reading 'noels', political parodies of carols, presumably (Nabokov, iii, 352).

16 – refers possibly to the Southern Society, organised by the Decembrist Pavel Pestel (see Brodskii; Lotman argues that the society alluded to may be the Soiuz Blagodenstviia, p. 207).

17 – refers to all this revolutionary activity as the 'idleness of young minds'.

Morozov's version differs from the above; it did not contain the fourth line of stanza 14 (referring to 'cautious I′ia'), and omitted the entire 17th stanza, as well as 11 lines in each of the 15th and 16th stanzas. The existence of three 'draft' stanzas, which supply the full 15th, 16th and 17th stanzas, has been debated. Initially V.I. Sreznvskii, who continued the archiving work on Pushkin's papers begun by L.N. Maikov, who died in 1904, labelled these verses part of 'Onegin's Journey'. However, these missing verses appear in most versions (Brodskii, Nabokov) and have been generally accepted as part of the missing chapter, if indeed there is such; some critics still dispute the existence of the 10th Chapter. It has been suggested that these fragments belong to the novel as a whole, that the first line would appear to fit clearly into Chapter IV, stanza 36 (Kozhevnikov, 1988: 265, a view supported by V. Turbin in an afterword to Kozhevnikov's article in 1988, but disputed by A. Latsis), or arguing that the 10th Chapter may be an expurgated section of the 8th Chapter (D′iakonov, 1963) or was only an initial plan for the 7th Chapter (Tarkhova, 1978: 251).[66]

The revolutionary intent behind these fragments seems clear. Critics have, however, argued extensively over the exact placing of the stanzas. Nabokov separates stanza 10 into two, stanzas 10 and 11, thus giving him 18 (Nabokov, 1964: iii, p. 366). Lerner argued in 1913 over the placing of stanza 17, which should in his view go before 15, a point of view contradicted by critics who agree that it should remain the final stanza.[67] Brodskii (1932: 195f.) numbers the stanzas differently, arguing for 16 in total with the merging of 13 and 14 as stanza 13: 1, 2, 3, 4, 8, 6, 9, 10, 5, 11, 12, 17, 13 (inc. 14), 15, 6, 7. Ultimately such a question can only be of relative value, as the verses exist in such an unfinished form; whether Pushkin would have altered them radically or indeed rejected them entirely, had he finished and been able to publish the 10th Chapter, remains one of the many hypotheses surrounding these 17 fragments. The questions raised by the fact of their existence are: how seriously was the novel affected by the problem of censorship? – an unanswerable query, and secondly, can the text in fact be regarded as complete (a question addressed in Part II of this study).

Tat'iana's dream

One active sub-school of Onegin criticism has focussed on Tat'iana's dream. Katz in 1980 offered an overview article, in which he discussed Cizevsky's interest in the symbols within the dream (1953), an approach based on the idea that Pushkin might have been influenced by G.H. von Schubert's *Die Symbolik des Traumes* (published in Russia in translation in 1814. He provided a useful discussion of the number of times, and contexts within which the words 'mechta' and 'son' appear in the text.[68] Other critics have approached the dream in ways which can be broadly classified as either (1) chronological, the dream is seen as both or either a reflection of the past, particularly of the ball, or as a foreshadowing of the name-day party and duel; (2) as intertextual, in terms of which critics have looked for the sources of the dream imagery; or (3) as psychological, arguing that the dream gives greater insight into the character of Tat'iana.

Critics who have adopted the first two approaches have provided no real key insights to the text as the whole, although they have offered valuable information, for example, pointing out certain links between the dream and Tat'iana's letter to Onegin (Samarin, 1927), suggesting that it is a recapitulation of the ball (Tangl, 1956), or linked to the rejection scene in the garden (Matlaw, 1959). Others have argued that the dream is principally prophetic (Blagoi, 1931), and therefore that the 'bear' refers to her future husband (Miller, 1899), while Nabokov (1964) has preferred to state that the dream is descriptive of both past and future. A second group of critics has pointed out the allusions made in the dream sequence to folklore (Gukovskii, 1957, Slonimskii, 1959, Grechina, 1978, and Hellberg, 1989), to myths (Markovich, 1981), to Tat'iana's reading (Stilman, 1958, Mitchell, 1968, Todd, 1978); to visual works such as the *liubok* and Bosch (Botsianovskii, 1921), to Dante and J. Malfilâtre (Picchio, 1976), to the dream of Sonia from Griboedov's *Gore ot uma* (Brodskii, 1957, Matlaw, 1959), and to Zhukovskii's *Svetlana* (Ryan & Wigzell, 1992). A more interesting approach has been V.S. Nepomniashchii's study of Dostoevskiian heroes in relation to the dream

(1982), an idea taken up by Bocharov, who likens Onegin to Dostoevskii's Stavrogin (1991: 179-80; 183), while M.G. Iskrin has taken a brief but different linguistic approach (1989).

More fruitful has been the psychoanalytical approach. Nesaule's claim that the dream is the 'key' to Tat'iana's soul (Nesaule, 1968: 124) and the belief that the dream shows Tat'iana's subconscious insight into the hero (Gershenzon, 1926)[69] was developed by Matlaw in terms of the value of the dream as indicative of the heroine's vacillating states of fear and trust towards Onegin (Matlaw, 1959: 490) by Gregg in a Freudian analysis (1969) which discusses Tat'iana's frightened erotic fascination with Onegin, and by Daniel Rancour-Laferrière (1989).

Clayton's feminist reading of the text has provided an interesting interpretation which neatly explains the reaction Tat'iana has to Onegin, her fascination with, and fear of, him, an aspect of the theme of negative eroticism which Pushkin describes in other texts. It also suggests why Onegin is portrayed as a 'killer'; he is the man who will 'destroy' Tat'iana's maidenly hopes and innocence (Clayton, 1987). A similar idea is suggested by Greenleaf, who points to the dream as a means of telling Tat'iana that she has a 'mixed animal and human nature', which in its violence and cruelty is contorted to the 'false romanticism' of Lenskii and Ol'ga. Tat'iana's dream takes the reader on a typical 'Onegin journey' – one from certainty to a state of dreamlike unknowing. It emphasises the lack of understanding that the characters demonstrate of their own natures, of their actions, and of the nature of reality – whatever that is – itself.

Notes to Part One

1. The article is given in Zelinskii, II: 11-16. The reference to 'nekotorye kritiki' is on p. 15. The response to Polevoi which appeared in *Moskovskii Telgraf* in 1825, suggesting that Polevoi's defence should wait until more of the novel had been published, appears in Zelinskii, II: 17-23.

2. Although see F. Bulgarin's comments on Onegin's 'opaqueness', and unsatisfactory nature as a protagonist, from an article in *Severnaia pchela* 132 (1926), quoted in Zelinskii, II: 41f.

3. See an article by N.N. in *Moskovskii vestnik* VIII, 4 (1828): 'snom Tat'iany voskhishchaiutsia vse' (Zelinskii, II: 79).

4. For a detailing of the exact date and place of publication of the separate chapters of *Evgenii Onegin*, see V. Nabokov's *Eugene Onegin*, I: 74-83.

5. Bulgarin's motivation for the hostile review does not bear close analysis, as Clayton explains (Clayton, 1985: 15), for it seems likely that Bulgarin was reacting to a negative review (which he wrongly attributed to Pushkin) of one of his own novels.

6. See Rainer Grübel's comments on Gogol's and Turgenev's views of Pushkin: 'Convention and Innovation of Aesthetic Value: The Russian Reception of Aleksandr Pushkin', in Theo D'haen, Rainer Grübel & Helmut Lethen, (eds.), *Convention and Innovation in Literature* (Amsterdam/ Philadelphia, Benjamins, 1989), 181-224.

7. Sona Hoisington's translation of Belinskii's 1845 article on Tat'iana appears in *Canadian-American Slavic Studies* XXIX, 3-4 (1995), 371-94.

8. See D. I. Pisarev, 'Pushkin i Belinskii: Evgenii Onegin', in his *Sochineniia*, III (Moscow, GiKhl, 1956), 306-64. For a detailed examination of Pisarev's attack, see J. Forsyth's 'Pisarev, Belinsky and *Yevgeniy Onegin*', *Slavic and East European Review* 48 (1970), 163-80. Forsyth quotes from a rather nice letter by Anton Chekhov in 1892 on Pisarev's views, pp. 164-5.

9. F. M. Dostoevskii, 'Pushkin. Ocherk. Proizneseno 8 iuniia vzasedanii Obshchestva liubitelei rossiiskoi slovesnosti', in Dostoevskii, *Dnevnik pisatelia na 1877 god* (Paris, YMCA Press, undated), 510-27.

10. See the highly flattering volume of poetry dedicated to Pushkin which appeared in 1899, *Russkie poety o Pushkine* (Moscow, Tip. G. Lissnera & A. Geshelia, 1899). See also Levitt, p. 160 on the 'vulgarisation' of Pushkin during the 1899 celebration.

11. See Marshall Shatz's brief note on, and English translation of, this article by Kliuchevskii in *Canadian-American Slavic Studies* XVI, 2 (1982), 227-46.

12. See. D. N. Ovsianiko-Kulikovskii, *Voprosy psikhologii tvorchestva* (St. Petersburg, Izd. D.E. Zhukovskogo, 1902), 1-76 for a discussion of Tat'iana's 'Russianness', 26-8.

13. As Beatrice van Sambeek-Weideli notes in her listing of dissertations published between 1940 and 1982, the bias towards realist interpretations of the text remains strong (van Sambeek-Weideli, 1989: 399).

14. B. L. Modzalevskii, 'Biblioteka Pushkina: Bibliograficheskoeopisanie', *Pushkin i ego sovremenniki*, 9-10 (St. Petersburg, imp.Ak. Nauk, 1910), pp. 1-442; an addendum was published in 1934 in *Literaturnoe nasledstvo*.

15. See his section 'Pushkin ob "Onegine"', and the section dealing with the prevalence of words such as 'blesk' and 'blestit'' in the novel. N. Brodskii, *Komentarii k romanu A.S. Pushkina "Evgenii Onegin"* (Moscow, Mir, 1932), 176-7.

16. B. Eikhenbaum, 'Problemy poetiki Pushkina', written 1921, first published 1924; see his *O poezzii* (Leningrad, Sovetskii pisatel', 1969), pp. 23-34: 'Do sikh por Pushkin byl slishkom blizok nam...My govorili o nem shkol'nym mertvym iazykom', p. 23.

17. See Maiakovskii's poem 'Iubileinoe' (1924), in which he gives the following mocking 'rewriting' of Onegin's letter to Tat'iana: 'Deskat', muzh u vas durak i staryi merin, ia liubliu vas, bud'te obiazatel'no moia, ia seichas zhe utrom dolzhen byt' uveren, chto s vami dnem uvizhus' ia'.

18. K. Simonov, 'Aleksandr Sergeevich Pushkin', in *A.S. Pushkin vrusskoi kritike* (Moscow, Khudozhestvennaia literatura, 1953), pp. 577-608 (p. 603). This dictum, that Pushkin was the 'first realist', was also propounded by Gukovskii in 1946 (his text was only published posthumously in 1957).

19. See J.T. Shaw's analysis of Vinogradov's study in 'Recent Soviet Scholarly Books on Pushkin: A Review Article', *Slavic and East European Journal*, X, 1 (1966), 66-84 (p. 78).

20. Although V.A. Grekhnev in his 'Dialog s chitatelem v romane Pushkina *Evgenii Onegin*', in Pushkin. *Issledovaniia i materialy* ix (Leningrad, Nauka, 1979), pp. 100-9, develops the Bakhtinian polyphonic idea.

21. There is a posthumous publication by Lotman, *Pushkin* (St. Petersburg, Iskusstvo-SPB, 1995), containing his commentary on *Onegin* as well as additional, new material.

22. The reader will find a brief introduction in English to Lotman's thoughts on this subject in J.M. Lotman, 'Point of View in a Text', *New Literary History* VI, 2 (Winter, 1975), 339-52.

23. A study which does not go far enough down this line, but which suggests another way of approaching it, is N. Solovei's 1981 monograph, which devotes fair attention to the contradicting lyric and epic voices in the text. N. Ia. Solovei, *Roman A.S. Pushkina 'Evgenii Onegin'* (Moscow, Vysshaia shkola, 1981).

24. V. Lakshin, 'Dvizhenie "svobodnogo romana": Zametki o romane *Evgenii Onegin*', *Literaturnoe obozrenie* 6 (1979), 17-24.

25. V.N. Turbin, 'Romanist i roman', in his *Pushkin, Gogol, Lermontov* (Moscow, Proshveshchenie, 1978), 177-90. I am grateful to Michael Pursglove for bringing this article to my attention.

26. Clayton labels Bocharov structuralist (1986: 64), but Hoisington calls him phenomenological (1988: 25). Briefly, structuralist critics analyse literature on the basis of linguistic theory and the linguistic/literary conventions and codes that constitute the 'mode of writing' which is a literary text. Phenomenological critics analyse the forms of consciousness embodied in the work both by the author and by the 'active reader'.

27. S.G. Bocharov, *Poetika Pushkina: ocherki* (Moscow, Nauka,1974), 26-104.

28. See V. Buznik, 'Mera klassiki – gumanizm', *Russkaia literatura* 3 (1987), p. 4.

29. Those interested in this alleged major literary find can consult M.I.P. Company, Minneapolis, who printed the book in Russian in 1986; it has been translated into seven other languages. See the MIP webpage at http://www.mipco.com/MiP.html.

30. I. Murav'eva, 'Vot moi Onegin', *Grani*, 144 (1987), 63-83.

31. V.N. Turbin, '"On vidit bashnuiu Godunova...". Motivy i obrazy dramy A.S. Pushkina "Boris Godunov" v romane "Evgenii Onegin"', *Vestnik moskovskogo universiteta. Seriia 9, Filologiia*, 9, No. 3 (1987), 3-7.

32. V.S. Baevskii, 'Tematicheskaia kompozitsiia "Evgeniia Onegina" (Priroda i funktsii tematicheskikh povtorov)', in *Pushkin: issledovaniia i materialy*, 13 (1989), 33-44.

33. M.G. Iskrin, 'Gadatel', tolkovatel' snov', *Russkaia rech'*, 3 (1989), 140-4.

34. V.S. Solov'eva, 'Sravneniia v romane A.S. Pushkina "Evgenii Onegin"', *Russkii iazyk v shkole* 3 (1989), 73-8, and L.G. Barlas, 'O kategorii vyrazitel'-nosti, i izobrazitel'nykh sredstvakh iazyka', *Russkii iazyk v shkole* 1 (1989), 75-80. See also M.S. Berezhkova, 'Ekspressiia oneginskoi strofy', *Russkii iazyk vshkole*, 5 (1982), 48-52.

35. N.I. Mikhailova, 'Roman "Evgenii Onegin" i oratorskaia kul'tura pervoi treti XIX v', in *Pushkin. Issledovaniia i materialy*, 13 (1989), 45-62.

36. S. Bocharov, S., 'Frantsuzskii epigraf k Evgeniiu Oneginu', *Cahiers du monde russe et soviétique* 32, No. 2 (1991), 173-88.

37. V. Baevskii, V., *Skvoz' magicheskii kristal. Poetika 'Evgeniia Onegina', romana v stikhakh A. Pushkina* (Moscow, Prometei, 1990). This text, which originally appeared in shortened form, in *Literaturnaia Rossiia* in 1988, is also reproduced in Turbin's *Nezadolgo do Vodoleia* (Moscow, Radiks, 1994).

38. V.I. Matsapura, 'Podrazhaniia "Evgeniiu Oneginu" na Ukraine (20-40e gody XIX)', *Voprosy russkoi literatury: republikanskii mezhvedomstvennyi nauchnyi sbornik*, 2 (56) (1990), 113-21.

39. Nishikov, Iu. M., '"Evgenii Onegin": Geroi i istoriia: Etapy stanovleniia istorizma v pushkinskom romane', *Izvestiia Akademii Nauk, Seriiia literatury i iazyka*, 50, No. 4 (1991), 314-27

40. Makhov, A.E., '"Magicheskii kristal" A.S. Pushkina i "Volshebnyi khrystalek" N.M. Konshina', *Russkaia rech'*, 3 (1991), 3-7.

41. N.I. Khardzhiev, 'Kratkaia istoriia "vina komety"', *Russkaia rech'* 4 (1991), p. 8, and M.G. Iskrin, 'Otryvki severnikh poem', *Russkaia rech'* 3 (1990), 18-20.

42. S. Freilikh, 'Parodiia kak priem: O Pushkine i Eizenshteine', *Voprosy literatury* 5 (1991), 117-43.

43. S.A. Fomichev, 'U istokov oneginskogo zamysla', *Russkaia rech'* 1 (1992), 10-14.

44. Iu. Lotman, 'Smert' kak problema siuzheta', in V. Polukhina, J. Andrew & R. Reid (eds.), *Literary Tradition and Practice in Russian Culture. Papers from an International Conference on the Occasion of the Seventieth Birthday of Yury Mikhailovich Lotman* (Amsterdam/Atlanta, Rodopi; Series in Slavic Literature and Poetics, 1993), 1-15

45. V. Turbin, 'Evgenii Onegin i M"y' (sic), *The Pushkin Journal* 1, No. 2 (1993), 197-212. Turbin's 1996 (posthumous) publication of his 1987 dissertation (deemed unacceptable for publication at that time), (*Poetika romana A.S. Pushkina 'Evgenii Onegin'*, Moscow, Mos. universitet, 1996) appeared too late for comment.

46. See the description of this project in 'Vtoraia mezhdunarodnaia pushkinskaia konferentsiia', *Russkaia literatura* 3 (1993), 209-20, p. 217, and in N.I. Mikhailova, 'Oneginskaia entsiklopediia: Ot zamysla k vosploscheniiu', *Oktiabr'* 2 (1995), 162-76.

47. Which appeared in *New Republic*, 89 (9 December, 1936); it was later rewritten for republication in 1952.

48. Although the work of the Italian scholar Ettore Lo Gatto on the novel, three articles which appeared in 1955, 1958 and 1962, had already been assessed by Stanley Mitchell in 1966. J. Thomas Shaw had also looked at another aspect of critical reception in his 1966 article on Soviet books on *Onegin*.

49. See. V. Setschkareff's discussion of the difference between the sentimental novel and the Byronic picaresque/epic, in *Alexander Puschkin: Sein Leben und Sein Werk* (Wiesbaden, Otto Harrassowitz, 1963).

50. Fanger's chapter also provides an analysis of the artistic relationship between Pushkin and Gogol.

51. J.D. Clayton, 'Evgenii Onegin: v poiskakh fabuly', *Russian Literature* 23-3 (October, 1988), 303-18, p. 315. This article has been published in Russian only; the translation is my own.

52. T. Barran, 'Who Killed Lensky? The Narrator as Assassin in *Eugene Onegin*', in *Selected Proceedings of the Kentucky Foreign Language Conference: Slavic Section*, v, No. 1 (1987-8), 7-15.

53. Melchior D. Wolff, 'Romanticism Unmasked: Lexical Irony in Aleksandr Puskin's *Evgenij Onegin', in Convention and Innovation in Russian Literature*, 361-88. A recent edition of *Canadian-American Slavic Studies* devoted to Russian Romanticism included two articles on *Onegin* – but both were translations of earlier texts – Sona Hoisington's translations of an article by I.N. Semenko from 1957 on the author in *Onegin*, which argues for the text as an 'indivisible whole', appears in *CASS* 29, Nos. 3-4 (1995), 233-57; Hoisington's translation of Belinskii's 1845 article on Tat'iana appears in the same volume, pp. 371-94.

54. 'Antenantiosis' is a somewhat recondite critical term, similar to the better-known concept of litotes, i.e. the assertion of an affirmative by negating its contrary (i.e. 'he's not the brightest'); antenantiosis is 'a positive statement made in a negative form'.

55. Patricia Roosevelt, 'Tat'iana's Garden: Noble Sensibilities and Estate Park Design in the Romantic Era', *Slavic Review* 49, no. 3 (Fall, 1990), 335-49 (pp. 347-50).

56. W.F. Ryan, and F. Wigzell, 'Gullible Girls and Dreadful Dreams. Zhukovskii, Pushkin and Popular Divination', *Slavonic and East European Review*, 70, No. 4 (October, 1992), 647-69).

57. M.C. Levitt, 'Pushkin Pro Semiosis: The Dialectic of the Sign in Canto One *of Evgenii Onegin', Russian Literature* 34-4 (1993), 439-50.

58. R. Tempest, 'The Girl on the Hill: Parallel Structures in *Pride and Prejudice* and *Eugene Onegin', Elementa: Journal of Slavic Studies and Comparative Cultural Semiotics*, I, 2 (1993), 197-213.

59. J. Garrard, 'Corresponding Heroines in "Don Juan" and "Evgenii Onegin"', *Slavonic and East European Review* 73, No. 3 (1995), 428-48.

60. See T. Miller and M.S. Boyd (tr.), 'Lermontov Reads *Eugene Onegin', The Russian Review*, 53, No. 1 (1994), 59-66.

61. Emerson, C., 'Tat'iana' in *A Plot of her Own. The Female Protagonist in Russian Literatur*e (ed. S. Hoisington) (Evanston, Northwestern UP, 1995).

62. See N.E. Downey, *The Garden in the Graveyard: Memory in Pushkin's* '*Evgeny Onegin*', (unpublished dissertation, Brown University, 1995); the abstract can be found in *Dissertation Abstracts International*, LV, 9 (March, 1995), 285A-59A.

63. Although her idea that the text seeks to create a reader-author common ground of 'the spiritual mobility of Romantic irony' (Greenleaf, 1994: 17) requires more explication. Greenleaf's book developed the more limited ideas of B.M. Zhirmunskii (1924); the latter discussed Pushkin's debt to the English Romantic poet. B.M. Zhirmunskii, *Bairon i Pushkin* (Leningrad, Academia, 1924).

64. Surprisingly, Clayton barely mentions the debate on the 10th Chapter in his critical history. See P.O. Morozov, 'Shifrovannoe stikhotvorenii Pushkina' in *Pushkin i ego sovremenniki* (St. P., 1910, ed. 13).

65. N. Eidel'man, '*Evgenii Onegin*: The mystery of the tenth chapter', originally in *Literaturnaia gazeta* 1974, No. 23, reprinted in *Soviet Studies in Literature* xi, No. 1 (Winter 1974-5), 8-15 offers a useful, if rather rhetorical, overview of the history of scholarship on the chapter from Morozov's discovery until 1974.

66. See V. Kozhevnikov, 'Shifrovannye strofy "Evgeniia Onegina"', *Novyi mir* 6 (1988), and his 'Imela li mesto "rasseiannost'"?', *Novyi mir* 6 (1989), 268-9, in response to A. Latsis, '"Dikie utki", i ne tol'ko!', *Voprosy literatury* 12 (1988), 254-59.

67. N. O. Lerner, 'Iz desiatoi (sozzhenoi) glavy "Evgeniia Onegina"', in *Pushkin. Sochineniia* (ed. S.A. Vengerov) (P., 1915), vol. 6, and 'Novye priobreteniia pushkinshogo teksta i dopolneniia. Iz desiatoi (sozhzhennoi) glavy "Evgeniia Onegina"', in *Pushkin* (Brockhaus-Efron, 1915); and M.L. Gofman, 'Propushchennye strofy "Evgeniia Onegina" in vol 6 of *Pushkin. Sochineniia*. Other comments on the 10th chapter can be found in: D.N. Sokolov, 'Po povodu shifrovannogo stikhotvoreniia Pushkina, in *Pushkin i ego sovremennki*, vi (Petersburg, Ross. gos akad. tip., 1922); B. Tomashevskii, 'Desiataia glava "Evgeniia Onegina"', *Literaturnoe nasledstvo* 16-18 (1934), 379-80; and N. D'iakonov, 'O vos'moi, deviatoi i desiatoi glavakh "Evgeniia Onegina"', *Russkaia literatura* 3 (1963), 259-66.

68. See Clayton as well on this lexical subject, p. 204 (footnote 25), and, p. 183 and p. 204 (footnotes 22 & 23), on the kinds of dreams to be found in the work.

69. There is a translation of Gershenzon's 1926 work on the subject – see his 'Dreams in Pushkin', *Russian Literature Triquarterly* 24 (Spring, 1990), 163-176.

Part Two: The Text

Translations and commentaries

The Russian text most readily available is A.S. Pushkin, *Evgenii Onegin* (ed. A. Briggs) (BCP Russian Texts, 1993), which also contains a useful Introduction.

Evgenii Onegin, like all Russian poetry, poses particular problems for translators, who find themselves torn between the demands of linguistic exactitude and the desire to reproduce the stylistic elegance of the work, created largely by its metre and rhyme scheme. The first approach is the one adopted by Vladimir Nabokov (see below), whose literal translation, though most unpoetic and at times rather old-fashioned, is usefully exact and explanatory.[1] Of the remaining English translations (there are no fewer than twelve in all – see the *Bibliography*), the most recent, James Falen's 1995 edition, replicates the rhyming lines, although in rendering the language rather too modern and American, Falen's translation is perhaps less satisfying than the more old-fashioned yet sonorous translation by Charles Johnston.[2] The novel has been translated into several other languages, including Dutch, Greek and Polish.[3]

Of the *Commentaries*, Nabokov's is the most extensive, if at times rather eccentric. The only other English commentary in existence is Cizevky's, which is much more brief, but which contains the Russian text as well, all in one volume. Of the Russian commentaries, the best is Lotman's, as Brodskii's tends to be rather clumsily sociological in places. Mikhailova's work is not a full commentary by any means, but is included here because the study follows a chapter-by-chapter structure; the material is presented in rather a disjointed manner, however.

Cizevsky, D., *Evgenij Onegin* (Cambridge, Harvard University Press, 1953)
Brodskii, N.L., *Komentarii k romanu A. S. Pushkina 'Evgenii Onegin'* (Moscow, Mir, 1932)
Lotman, Iu. M., *Roman A.S. Pushkina 'Evgenii Onegin'* (Leningrad, Prosveschenie, 1980)
Mikhailova, N.I., *Sobranie pestrykh glav* (Moscow, Imidzh, 1994)

These Commentaries will be referred to during the following brief explication of each chapter, as an indication to readers that further detail is available on certain significant points.

A cast list

(The list excludes references to literary figures unless they appear as characters, rather than as literary allusions, or figures of comparison i.e. Onegin as Chadaaev in I, 25)

The narrator (unnamed): a friend of Onegin's

Evgenii Onegin: a cynical nobleman

Onegin's uncle: whose estate Evgenii inherits; he dies in Chapter 1

Tat'iana Dmitrievna Larina: our heroine, a Romantic young girl

Ol'ga Dmitrievna Larina: her younger sister, a pragmatist

Vladimir Lenskii: a 17-year-old Romantic young man, engaged to Ol'ga, and Onegin's neighbour and friend

Madame Praskovia Larina: the girls' mother, and (like Tat'iana) an admirer of Richardson's romances

Dmitrii Larina: landowner, *brigadir*, and her husband, who dies in chapter 2

Tat'iana's nurse Filip'evna[4]

Princess Alina: Madame Larina's cousin in Moscow

an unnamed general: 'Prince N.', Tat'iana's eventual husband

Zaretskii: Lenskii's second during the duel

Guillot: Onegin's French valet, and his second during the duel

country gentry and neighbours (such as young Dunia, II, 12): or the guests at Tat'iana's name-day party (Pustiakov, Gvozdin, Skotininy, Petushkov, Buianov, Flianov, Kharlikov, Triquet, the *rotnyi komandir*)

other minor characters: Madame (Onegin's nurse); Monsieur l'Abbé (Onegin's tutor); an *ulan* who marries Ol'ga; Anis'ia, Onegin's housekeeper; the hussar Pykhtin (who offers for Tat'iana); a *kalmyk,* servant to Princess Alina; Tat'iana's relations (Elena, Lukeria, Liubov', Ivan, Semen, Pelageia, and their daughters; M'sieur Finemouche (probably a tutor), Prolasov.

friends and contemporaries of Pushkin's: Petr Kaverin (hussar and socialite); Dunia Istomina (the dancer); Nikolai Iazykov (poet and acquain-tance); Zizi (Evpraksiia Vul'f, a lover); Evgenii Baratynskii (poet and friend); Anton Delvig (poet and close friend); Petr Viazemskii (poet and friend); Gavrila Derzhavin (the poet who 'discovered' Pushkin), Aleksandr Shiskov, Pavel Katenin, Adam Mickiéwicz[5]

contemporary references (apart from literary figures): the watchmaker Bréguet, the St. Petersburg restaurateur Talon, the Parisian restaurateur Very, the gunsmith Lepage, the artist Count F.P. Tolstoi, the caricaturist Saint-Priest

A Chronology of events (according to the old calendar)[6]

Date	Event	Chapter reference
1796	Onegin's birth	
1811/12	Onegin enters society	
1817/18-20	Lenskii studies in Göttingen	
1819-20	Onegin meets Pushkin[7]	Chapter I
summer 1820	Onegin meets Lenskii	Chapter II
summer 1820	Onegin meets Tat'iana	
January 5, 1821 (Epiphany Eve)	Tat'iana's dream	Chapter V
January 12, 1821	Tat'iana's name-day party	Chapter V
January 14, 1821	The duel; Lenskii dies	Chapter VI
	Ol'ga marries	Chapter VII
July 3, 1821	Onegin leaves Petersburg	Chapter VII
Jan./Feb 1822	Tat'iana is taken to Moscow	Chapter VII
Autumn 1822	Tat'iana marries	
Autumn 1823	Onegin and the author meet in Odessa	
August 1824	Onegin returns and sees Tat'iana	Chapter VIII
winter 1824/5	Onegin reads, reclusively	Chapter VIII
February 1825	Onegin and Tat'iana meet again	Chapter VIII

Commentary to *Evgenii Onegin*

The title, epigraph and preface

The epigraph to the novel, rather misleadingly labelled 'tiré d'un lettre particulière', was written by Pushkin himself in 1823. Initially the epigraph to the first chapter, it was later elevated to the status it now occupies.[8] It is worth quoting in full (in translation for the benefit of readers whose French may be a little rusty):

> Filled with vanity, he was yet distinguished by that particular pride which forces one to admit to good and bad acts with equal indifference – the consequence of a feeling of superiority, probably imaginary.

Pushkin's statement appears clear in intent; he will set out to describe a man who, although capable of good, is incapable of accepting his own subjection to moral laws. Onegin is not so much a superfluous man as a superman (as Bocharov has argued, perhaps a prototype for Dostoevskii's Stavrogin in *Besy*, Bocharov, 1991: 183). This epigraph is of particular significance in the understanding of a text which, despite critics' suggestions, was called by its author 'Evgenii Onegin' (and not 'Tat′iana Larina', or 'the diary of a superfluous man', or 'love, duels and disillusionment' or 'a Russian Childe Harold'). If he is defined as a superman, Onegin's killing of his friend Lenskii in a duel takes on its proper significance; it is an attempt to conquer weak feelings. As in Dostoevskii's *Prestuplenie i nakazanie,* when, after murdering the moneylender, Raskol′nikov realises that his conscience will not let him lie, Onegin is brought to a feeling of humility through the medium of Tat′iana, that epitome of the Russian soul, and now Onegin's 'conscience'. She later denies herself to him out of loyalty – the loyalty which Onegin did not show to his friend Lenskii when he set out to tease, humiliate and finally kill him.

The prefatory piece first appeared in 1828 (the separate edition of Chapters IV and V), before being transferred to its present position with the omission of the words 'To Petr Aleksandrovich Pletnev'.[9] The verse (of 17 lines, not the usual 14) offers some thoughts on the kind of novel Pushkin was offering his readers: a 'collection of variegated chapters' ('sobran′e pestrykh glav', line 10), in the well-known phrase; his text would be half-humorous, half-sad, plain yet idealistic, the fruit both of light and serious labour, of emotion and intellect. Pushkin gives warning to his readers that they will, indeed, find a text of contrasts and paradoxes, a novel filled with internal tensions and opposing moods, a 'novel in verse', as the subtitle states, combining both the prosaic and the poetic.

Chapter I: A rake's progress

The epigraph to this chapter is from a poem by Viazemskii, 'Pervyi sneg', 1816-19, pub. 1822), whose presence is felt thrice more in the text (V: 3; VII: 1, VII: 49), and refers to Viazemskii's metaphor in which a sleigh ride is compared to youth which, ardent, hurries to live, hastens to feel. As well as introducing one of the many references to the passing of time, Pushkin offers a standard Romantic image of the impatient, feeling soul, expecting, no doubt, that life will offer it something wonderful; but does it? Both Onegin and Tat'iana are offered love, but don't take it. It immediately becomes clear that the romantic worldview is a central theme to this text.

As Romanticism (and 'romanticism') will be referred to frequently in the following chapter summaries, it is as well to state, briefly, what is meant by the terms 'Romantic' and 'romantic', which have already been used in the preceding section (Part I) in respect of 20th-century critical views on Pushkin's romanticism (see my comments on Ivanov-Razumnik, Lavrin, Vickery, Wollf and Greenleaf). It was John Bayley who stated that for Pushkin Romanticism was a literary technique, not a personal feeling (Bayley, 1971: 91), and *Onegin*, with its parallels with Byron's *Don Juan* (1819-24), is mainly concerned with mocking the 'purple', i.e. rather overblown poetic effusions to which poets of the cult of sensibility were often prone, as well as the over-used and therefore increasingly trite conventions of much Sentimental and Romantic literature. Briefly, such conventions entailed, naturally, love scenes and amatory interludes, epistolary effusions (Richardson's texts being the prime example of this type), a beautiful and virtuous heroine, a hero given either towards passion or gloom (or both, as in the case of Evgenii), escapism (particularly from the corrupt world of urban society), nature-worship, and, most importantly, an idealistic or 'romantic' worldview, in terms of which love is the aim of existence and the means of resolving all conflict and pain. However, Romanticism has, of course, two sides, and the opposite of such idealism is the disaffected, Byronic, satirical and ironic face of the man disappointed by life's inability to offer such resolution and harmony and who therefore retreats from the world and lives according to his own rules (hence the Napoleonic, or 'superman' theme which runs alongside the image of Cain, the archetypal Romantic outcast, in much Romantic literature).

Russian Romanticism incorporates many different facets, from the more Byronic strain associated with Lermontov and his cult of the 'superfluous man', to the revolutionary romanticism of the Decembrists, to the German-influenced nature philosophy of Tiutchev. Pushkin's attitude towards Romantic conventions can be summed up, as it frequently has been, by the word 'parody'; *Onegin* clearly shows the difficulty of imposing a literary and idealistic pattern on daily behaviour, an imposition which leads, arguably, in the case of Lenskii, to a duel and to death; Pushkin's 'mocking imitation' of a Romantic tale is directed towards exposure of the gap between reality and Romanticism. Towards the romantic worldview in a more general sense, Pushkin shows some ambivalence. He does not demonstrate a belief in nature philosophy, but has a keen love of nature; Schelling's concept of poetry as the highest form of cognition is an issue which is debated in *Onegin*, and the author shows the flaws in such a concept, while simultaneously trying through his poetry to discover truth. Romantic irony permeates Pushkin's texts, in terms of which the poet appears to become his own audience, commenting amusingly and watchfully on his own tendency towards sentiment. Ultimately, there is no escaping romanticism, despite the poet's critical attitude towards Romantic conventions,[10] for a strong reaction to the cult of sensibility is an admission of the great significance of that cult.[11] In the following summary, therefore, the parodic impulse directed against Romantic conventions coexists with a more complex awareness of the romantic dilemma.

Onegin is, although theoretically a typical Romantic hero, hastening towards life's pleasures, rather ironically hurrying towards death. Having learned that his uncle is failing fast, he leaves for the latter's country estate (Nabokov argues that the place is about 200 miles west of Moscow) with impatience and considerable boredom. Family feeling is markedly absent, as is stated in the humorous reference to a fable by Krylov ('The donkey was of the most high principles' – 'osel byl samykh chistykh pravil'). This defines the attitude of the young Onegin to his uncle (the 'donkey') very neatly. Onegin, it is clear, is only interested in his inheritance, and his ardour and impatience (the Romantic qualities expected of a hero, as suggested in the epigraph) are only for money. The type of a man of no morals is already becoming clear.[12] However, the amusing tone serves to make the reader feel not dismay, but a cynical appreciation of the honesty displayed in place of more conventionally hypocritical expressions of mourning.

Onegin, a youthful rake (a 'povesa', stanza 2; Pushkin also uses the word 'frant', or dandy, I: 25, to describe his hero), the son of a man noted only for giving balls thrice yearly (stanza 3), has been brought up without much sternness or moral severity, and sent out into the world of high society with only those social accomplishments deemed necessary, namely, the ability to speak French, to dance and to bow elegantly, and to keep up a fashionable appearance. In addition, Onegin has, by dint of offering of the odd epigram or Latin tag, and by knowing when to keep silent, learned the knack of appearing rather more learned than he in fact is. He also knows, the narrator tells us with some irony, a little about the economist Adam Smith – Onegin is, as we have already learned, interested in money. The reference in stanza 7 to the 'simple product' is an allusion to Smith's doctrine that raw materials were more important than actual money in calculating a country's wealth;

Onegin's father never understood the value of land, and consequently mortgaged the family estates.

Pushkin has started his story with a depiction of a rake's education common to many tales of the time; yet beneath the clichéd structure lies a deeper concern with what man 'knows': the superficiality of Onegin's knowledge will prove his downfall. Later, the duel scene will demonstrate Onegin's belief that appearances are more important than feelings; the duel may in itself be triggered by Onegin's embarrassment at Tat′iana's revealing her feelings for him at the preceding party. Onegin's later adoration of Tat′iana may simply stem from a desire to covet one whose appearance is consummately perfect, who is the epitome of what is proper ('du comme il faut').

Onegin's last-mentioned, and greatest accomplishment, is his ability to play the lover. To Evgenii it appears that love is only a game (as he later states, IV, stanza 7). The insincerity referred to in stanza 10 indicates that he is very far from feeling the passions described by Ovid (i.e. by Nazon, stanza 8). Instead, he appears to regard love purely in terms of conquest (the missing stanzas 13 and 14 also have motifs of conquering – see Nabokov II, 66-7) and delights in tricking husbands – he is a Faublas. This, the seducer-'hero' (of the 1787-90 novel by Louvet de Couvrai), is a character who delights in deflowering even his friends' loved ones (Nabokov, II, 63); Pushkin hints at the attention Evgenii will later pay to Ol′ga.

Stanzas 15-28 describe the typical life of a young gentleman-about-town, with late mornings, invitations to social events, promenades along Nevskii Prospekt, trips to the fashionable Talon's restaurant,[13] and to the theatre. Stanza 18 provides a listing of well-known theatrical people, from dramatists to the ballet-master Didelot (Cizevsky, 214-5) to see the ballet where Dunia Istomina twirls delightfully, like down puffed from the lips of the Greek god of the winds, Aeolus (see Baevskii, 1990, 58-64 or Nabokov, II, 86-90 for more about Dunia). Then there are the hours spent dressing for a ball – Evgenii, like Chaadaev (stanza 25), is distinguished by the elegance of his attire – and attending same. The narrator breaks off to address the reader directly in stanzas 29-34 on the subject of balls, on the passions aroused on these occasions, and in a famous digression, on those feelings aroused by women's feet. The owner of this particularly adored pair of feet is not known (see Nabokov, II, 120-35 for possibilities).

The narrator returns to Onegin in stanza 35, describing how for the young hero the social whirl soon became boring; in stanza 38 we discover that he has contracted 'khandra', i.e. ennui, and now, like Byron's disaffected Romantic protagonist, Childe Harold (stanza 38), has become socially alienated, weary of life, and sombre in mind. Omitting stanzas 39-41 (which have never been found, and may not have existed), Pushkin describes his hero's boredom with women, both noblewomen and ladies of pleasure, his lazy inability to write, and his dissatisfaction with books, which he finds lacking in helpful philosophy (stanza 44). Mikhailova has commented that this state of boredom contrasts strongly with the 'joking' atmosphere of this chapter (1994: 12); Onegin's 'khandra' seems a pose, rather than deep-rooted *accidie*. It is at this stage that he becomes friendly with the narrator/Pushkin, who is finding life equally stale (stanza 45). The narrator claims to enjoy Evgenii's saturnine epigrams and caustic arguments (stanza 46), and together they muse away the evenings in recollection of happier, younger days; Pushkin introduces the nostalgic mode which will later reappear in the novel, and around which the theme of life's transience is constructed.

The narrator and Evgenii both decide that it is time to go abroad, as two Romantic stanzas, expressing a Byronic yearning for escape, suggest, (stanzas 49-50); but Onegin's plans are changed by the death of his father, the foreclosure by creditors on the Onegin estate, the death of his uncle and the inheritance by Evgenii of the latter's estate, the landscape of which quickly loses its charm and begins to bore him silly; the country, he finds, is just as dull as the city (stanza 54). This provides the major difference between Evgenii and the narrator (mentioned lest the reader might accuse the poet of having provided a self-portrait, stanza 56), who finds his greatest happiness whilst surrounded by the beauties of nature. The narrator does not, like Byron, write only 'about himself' ('o samom sebe', stanza 56). The question of whether he addresses his verses to any particular lady is the next issue, dealt with in stanza 57, in which Pushkin alludes to two of his own poems. The narrator then concludes the chapter with stanzas on the subject matter of his own verses (stanzas 57-60), introducing the metafictional notion of commenting on his own first chapter to date (stanza 60). The narrator, unlike Evgenii, has found something to do – i.e. write his novel in verse.

Chapter II: Romantic types: Lenskii, Tat'iana, Praskovia[14]

The two epigraphs to this Chapter allow Pushkin to play on the similarity between the Latin word for countryside (*rus*) and the old word for Russia, *Rus'*. Life in the Russian countryside is, indeed, the focus of this chapter, and provides a strong contrast to the city life which Evgenii has enjoyed, and which Tat'iana will later be forced to enter. Pushkin describes the estate to which Evgenii has succeeded, and the beauties of the grand old manor – attractions which cannot, however, stimulate the jaded palate of the hero. Evgenii does act to introduce one liberal reform, substituting for the *barshchina* (unpaid labour owed by a serf to his owner) a light *obrok* (rent in lieu), which allowed the serf more time to earn his own money instead of working his owner's land (stanza 4). This progressive deed wins Evgenii few fans amongst the country gentry, who soon realise that Evgenii dislikes their company; they label him strange and boorish (even a freemason). One amongst his neighbours is more to his taste; the young Lenskii, just returned from Göttingen and stuffed with Kantian philosophy and Romantic dreams.

Pushkin devotes stanzas 6-13 to a depiction of the poet, written in the clichéd language which poets of the time loved to use, a style used later in the depiction of Lenskii's death (Chapter VI). Lenskii as yet remains 'unwithered' as a result of contact with the 'cold corruption' of the world ('Ot khladnogo razvrata sveta/Eshche uvianut' ne uspev', stanza 7). He is still filled with hope, believing that he will find his soulmate; his verse, inspired apparently by the Romantic ideas of Schiller and Goethe, is filled with lofty feelings, images of roses, distant lands, and of life's transience (at seventeen, not a subject about which he could know much, as the narrator suggests at the end of stanza 10). His worldview combines Romantic idealism and nature worship with a contradictory (yet quite normal for Romantic characters) strain of Byronic and slightly morbid questing. Lenskii's friendship with Onegin is a union of opposites; in the famous lines, they meet like 'wave and rock, poetry and prose, ice and flame' ('volna i kamen'/Stikhi i proza, led i plamen'', stanza 13). This is a friendship which is both close yet based on no real sympathy; they are like brothers, but have become so from boredom ('ot delat' nichego', stanza 13) – a hint here, perhaps at the later fate of their friendship. The hint is underlined in stanza 14, when the narrator interpolates a comment on the lack of brotherhood between men, who are all now rather 'Napoleonic' ('My vse gliadim v Napoleony'), or coldly exploitative. Onegin, rather a Napoleonic type himself, as the epigraph to the novel has hinted, smiles at Lenskii's *naïveté*, and enjoys their conversations on weighty matters of life (Rousseau is one subject of discussion, argues Nabokov, II, 252), Lenskii's recitation of northern poems,[15] and his effusions on the theme of passion, poured forth from a soul 'burning with virgin fire' ('sogretoi devstvennym ognem', stanza 20). Onegin likes to hear the 'restless language of strange passions' ('Strastei chuzhikh iazyk miatezhnyi', stanza 18); even now he is not totally deaf to passion.

Ol'ga Larina, it seems, is the object of Lenskii's love (stanzas 21-3), described in conventional terms with her blue eyes and flaxen hair, and as the 'standard heroine' of any romance, as the narrator suggests (stanza 23). Her elder sister, Tat'iana, is the subject of stanzas 24-29. The narrator, by first introducing us to her conventional sister, prepares us for the notion that his heroine is no cliché-wrapped doll; even her name is an unusual one for the heroine of a novel of sensibility (not being considered sufficiently 'noble'). The salient characteristics of her nature are drawn initially in terms of two negative statements which describe her as not as beautiful as her sister, Ol'ga. Tat'iana is 'wild, sad, silent/As a frightened woodland doe' ('dika, pechal'na, molchaliva/Kak lan' lesnaia boiazliva', stanza 25) and 'strange even to her family', spending hours in silent dreaming, admiring the beauty of the Russian countryside, or reading Romantic literature (Richardson and Rousseau, stanza 29), a love for which has probably been imparted to her by her mother, whose life up to the death of Tat'iana's father is described in stanzas 29-36.

Tat'iana's mother continues the theme which Pushkin has played with thus far in the text, contrasting the ardour of the romantic soul with a more prosaic level of reality. Tat'iana's mother Praskovia, when young, played the part of a heroine from a sentimental novel. She was at first in love, hopelessly, with a man not destined to be her husband. However, not too long after marriage and removal to Larin's estate, she soon settles down to a comfortable life; and, as the narrator tells us, demonstrates the maxim that habit is often a substitute for happiness ('privychka svyshe nam dana;/Zamena schastiiu ona', stanza 31 – a paraphrase of a comment of Chateaubriand's).

The stanzas dealing with Praskovia offer several minor, yet significant points. The two names of Lovelace and Grandison, protagonists of Richardson's *Clarissa Harlowe* and his *Sir Charles Grandison* (1748, 1753-4) appear in stanza 30, suggesting that the Romanticism, as symbolised by these two men, has a Janus face. Grandison is the epitome of virtue, whereas Lovelace turns out to be an abductor and rapist of the simperingly innocent Clarissa. Pushkin, describing Mme. Larina, also underlines the affectation associated with Romanticism: when younger, she and other girls would write sentimental verses to female friends in blood, refashion Russian names into French ones, lace themselves into tight corsets, and pronounce the Russian letter 'n' in a nasal way, like a French 'n' (stanza 33).[16] Such affected ways are soon forgotten when Praskovia becomes Mme. Larina and settles happily on her estate, the beloved of her quiet husband. The two live a simple life, observing old Russian customs, such as eating pancakes during Maslianitsa, the period before the Russian Easter fast, and showing their fondness for superstitious customs such as dish-divination songs ('podbliudnye pesni') and the Russian round dance or *khorovod*, as well as the practice of decorating the home with buttercups in remembrance of the dead on Trinity Day (the eighth Sunday after Easter – see Nabokov, II, 300-1).[17]

They are, apparently, quite happy until the death of Larin, whose epitaph is given in stanza 37. This is the cue for Pushkin to reintroduce Lenskii, now shown meditating on life's transience as he stares at Larin's tombstone and quotes from that quintessential play on mortality, *Hamlet*; that strain of Byronic morbidity has resurfaced. The chapter ends with the narrator's direct address to the reader to enjoy life while it lasts, for all must die – although he expresses a hope that the poet's verses and fame may live on after his death (stanzas 39-40).

Chapter III: True romance? Tat'iana's letter

The epigraph, from the 18th-century French poet Malfilâtre's lines on the nymph Echo, who pined away for love of Narcissus, himself in love with his own reflection, sets the ironic tone for the forthcoming passionate declaration. Tat'iana, like Echo, falls in love with someone whose egotism prevents him from returning it. There is also an ironic suggestion that Tat'iana is portrayed as a reflection (an 'echo') of her own reading; she is one who must be in love, simply because 'elle était fille'. Pushkin's theme of identity is conveyed neatly in a one-line epigraph.

The first stanzas, which display some technical virtuosity (Cizevsky, 234) sets the plot in motion – Onegin will go with his friend Lenskii to the Larins' that evening to see Lenskii's 'Phyllida', i.e. Ol'ga, likened to a heroine from bucolic poetry (Nabokov, II, 322). On the way home from this simple country entertainment (see Cizevsky on the custom of offering jam and water to guests, 235), Onegin asks which one of the sisters was Tat'iana – an ingenious question, for clearly he has been intrigued by her. He compares his friend's *amour* to a Van Dyke Madonna (stanza 5), pretty, but moon-faced and stupid; Onegin's taste has clearly been for the one who sat 'molchaliva, kak Svetlana' (see Mikhalilova for a listing of Tat'iana's character traits, and commentary on her silence, 40-3). Pushkin introduces the first reference to the sentimental poet Vasilii Zhukovskii's ballad *Svetlana* (1812), to which he will also refer in Chapter V. The ballad deals with the dreams of the young Svetlana who, like Tat'iana in Chapter V, engages in divination, hoping to see the face of her lover. A nightmare results, but Svetlana's lover, whom she has believed dead, returns to marry her, and all ends in bliss. The text, an adaptation of Gottfried Bürger's *Lenore* (1773), introduces the theme of the demon lover, in Svetlana's case a Gothic theme with a happy resolution.[18] Would that it could be so for Pushkin's heroine.

Tat'iana falls in love (stanza 7, line 6), partly as it seems expected – the neighbours have already matched her with Onegin. Pushkin uses the phrase 'Alkalo pishchi rokovoi' ('desired fateful food'), with the Church Slavonic verb *alkat'* (meaning 'to hunger for') giving the line a sonorous, emotional ring (stanza 7, line 11). Anyone, really would have done for this young, ardent girl; her 'soul awaited...someone' ('dusha zhdala...kogo-nibud', stanza 7, line 14) as Pushkin says wryly (Nabokov, however, finds this line 'flat', II, 337). Deeply in 'love', Tat'iana, naturally, turns to books; stanza 9 describes her reading – Rousseau's *Julie, ou La nouvelle Héloïse* (1761), Cottin's *Mathilde* (1805), *Valérie*, by de Krüdener (1803-4), Goethe's *Die Leiden des jungen Werthers* (1774), de Staël's *Delphine* (1802), and Richardson's *Clarissa Harlowe* (1748) and *Sir Charles Grandison* (1753-4). The novels share a common type of Romantic heroine, whether this be the beautiful Julie, who gives herself to her lover for one night before marrying old Wolmar (there are obvious parallels here

here with Tat'iana's daring letter in which she 'gives' herself to Onegin, and her later marriage), the prissy Mathilde (sister of Richard Coeur de Lion) unsuitably in love (see Lotman, p. 211), the delicate Valérie pursued by de Linar, Charlotte, with whom Werther is infatuated in Goethe's epistolary novel, Richardson's boringly saintly Clarissa,[19] heroine of yet another epistolary effusion, Harriet Byron in *Sir Charles Grandison*, or the moral Delphine, who gives up her lover because he is married. The moral lessons in these texts may suggest that Tat'iana's reading influences her life up until the end of the novel, when she rejects Onegin partly from moral scruples.

The heroes of these works are generally Romantic, passionate and virtuous (Saint-Preux in *Héloïse,* Malek-Adhel, a Moslem general who pursues Mathilde, the violently passionate de Linar, the weepingly sentimental Werther, the tortured Léonce in *Delphine*, the insufferably noble Sir Charles Grandison. The obvious man out is Lovelace in *Clarissa Harlowe* (Cizevsky's commentary is inaccurate in stating that Grandison is the hero of this novel, p. 237). In stanza 12, Pushkin has more to say about a romantic maiden's taste in heroes, suggesting that she is inflamed by the following types: vampires (a reference to Byron or to Polidori; see Nabokov, II, 352); Maturin's Melmoth (1820), a rather Faustian and infernal type; the eternal Jew (a popular figure in Romantic literature, i.e. an outcast, in the vein of other Romantic figures such as Cain and Childe Harold); the romantically wild Corsair (from Byron's poem of that name from 1813-4), and the hero of Nodier's *Jean Sbogar* (1818), leader of a band of outlaws. Pushkin juxtaposes two different types of the Romantic hero, one noble, one sinister, concluding with words about Byron's ability to conceal the unpalatable truth of these types – Byron 'Oblek v unylyi romantizm/I beznadezhnyi egoizm' (stanza 12, lines 13-14).[20]

After the 'reading stanzas' (9-12), the narrator interrupts with three stanzas of sympathy for his heroine, who is now tasting of the 'magical poison of desire' ('volshebnyi iad zhelanii,' stanza 15) and continues with a description of her sad state; she is driven by the 'yearning for love' ('toska liubvi', stanza 16), and tormented by moonlight. We see her, sleepless, talking to her nanny about the latter's first love, an unromantic tale of an arranged marriage which neatly counterpoints Tat'iana's own anguish (a romance 'arranged' by literary convention?). Tat'iana's sleepless night will produce the famous letter to Onegin, but before giving us this passionate missive, Pushkin draws out the suspense by interpolating ten verses (stanzas 22-31) on another topic. In these he talks of cold society beauties who have caused him to flee, for the message '*Ostav' nadezhdu navsegda*' ('Abandon hope, all ye who enter here', from Dante's *Inferno*, suggesting that such women are 'hellish') appears to be written across their brows.

In what way is Tat'iana 'more guilty' than these tormenting women, asks the narrator? (stanza 24). Is it the depth of her passion that is unforgivable?

(line 13). Pushkin suggests that pretend love is more palatable than the real thing. Another problem, he sighs, is that he must translate the letter which Tat'iana has, of course, written in French, the language of the noble class of that time (see Lotman, 221-4 on Tat'iana's language). This problem allows the narrator to interpolate a peevish comment on how Russian women should be forced to read in Russian (perhaps Tat'iana would, in fact, be less Romantic had she done so?), but how ridiculous to think of ladies with the weekly Russian magazine the *Blagonamerennyi* (*Well-meaner*) in their hands (stanza 27); this publication was not considered suitable for women because of its vulgarities (see Cizevsky, 241, and Brodskii, 106-8).

The narrator eventually brings himself to attempt a translation of the letter, having admitted that Gallicisms are as dear to him as the verses of the minor poet (who influenced Pushkin) Ippolit Bogdanovich (stanza 29). Noting that passionate verses such as Parny's (a reference to the well known French writer of sensuous verses) are now out of fashion (stanza 29), he notes that he would have liked to rely on the help of his friend Evgenii Baratynskii, 1800-1844 (the 'pevets pirov' of stanza 30, line 1) in his translation.[22]

So, finally, to the 79-line letter, this 'mad', 'fascinating' and 'injurious' ('bezumnyi', 'uvlekatel'nyi' and 'vrednyi', stanza 31, lines 7-8) outpouring of the heart, in the narrator's view a 'Freishütz', or fragment from a romantic (Weber) opera played by hesitant music students, as the narrator states deprecatingly. V. Sipovskii has argued that there is a strong link between the letter and Julie's effusions in *La nouvelle Héloïse;*[23] Nabokov notices similarities with this text and with *Valérie*, and with Constant's *Adolphe* (Nabokov, II, 389-94; he also refers, less convincingly, to Austen and Racine). However, the ardour comes through such artificiality, drawing a masterful portrait of a passionate girl who feels that her destiny has been charted. Moving from the formal mode of address to the intimate , i.e. from 'vy' to 'ty', stating 'I am yours' (line 34), Tat'iana pours out her feelings without holding back; Onegin has been sent 'by God' (line 37), and will be Tat'iana's 'preserver' ('khranitel'', line 38, repeated line 58) until she dies (a somewhat ironic choice of words). Tat'iana feels no doubt that he is 'the one', although the juxtaposition of her 'he is the one' ('vot on') with the next line, 'Not so?' ('Ne pravda l'?', line 47) offers an ironic hint to the contrary, unheeded by Tat'iana herself. She refers to her dream; was it he, a 'dear dream' who came to her and whispered 'words of hope'? (lines 53, 58). This comment foreshadows the dream Tat'iana is shortly to have, and which will be anything but comforting. This is also hinted at in Tat'iana's question, 'Who are you, my angel or preserver/Or a perfidious seducer?' ('Kto ty, moi angel li khranitel'/Ili kovarnyi iskusitel'?', lines 58-9). Is this all 'obman neopytnoi dushi!' (line 62), i.e, the 'deception of an inexperienced soul'? One fears that passion will not be the reward even of such a letter, fastened, as all love-letters should be, with a 'rozovaia oblatka', or pink seal (one is reminded of the ornate letter seal used in Pushkin's Romantic parody 'Metel'').

Tat'iana, having sent the letter on its way via her nanny's grandson, must wait until evening for Evgenii to arrive. Distraught, she runs to the garden, where she hears a song (inserted between stanzas 39-40). This serves to draw out the suspense as the reader waits for Onegin to appear; the song, being about love, more precisely, about maidens who entice a young lad into their circle, only to throw berries at him, offers an interesting counterpoint to the scene about to ensue. It also offers, as Lotman has noted (Lotman, 233), a stylistic viewpoint (folkloristic) which contrasts with Tat'iana's Romantic style, emphasising, once again, the different styles and worldviews in the novel.

Chapter IV: The first refusal

Onegin has appeared before Tat'iana in the final stanza, 41, of the previous Chapter, like a 'grim shadow', and Tat'iana stands before him as if 'scorched by fire' (stanza 41, lines 6-7). Beginning in stanza 7 (Pushkin's initial six stanzas on women were omitted in the complete editions), the narrator notes that women are fascinated by the unattainable; the less we love women, the more they like us (the narrator inserts a reference to Lovelace in stanza 7, line 12, reminding the reader of the cruel 'hero' of *Clarissa Harlowe*).

The epigraph, taken from a statement to be found in Mde de Staël's *Considérations de la Révolution française* (1818), made by Jacques Necker, an 18th-century politician refers to morality ('morality is in the nature of things'), suggesting that 'life', human beings, presumably, act according to ethical principles. Will Onegin do so? What would the moral course be? Evgenii, we are told, is bored and wearied by passionate effusion, and is now a cold-hearted, ennui-ridden man. Yet, reading Tat'iana's letter, Evgenii 'was moved' (stanza 11, line 2); passion revives in him – but he does not wish to deceive 'the trustfulness of an innocent soul' ('doverchivost' dushi nevinnoi', stanza 11, line 12). Hence his statement to Tat'iana that he was moved by her passion, but that he cannot consider a liaison, for he is not meant for domestic bliss (which he sees as 'limitation', 13, 1); he was 'not created for happiness' ('ne sozdan dlia blazhenstva', stanza 14, line 1). He can offer her only a brotherly love (stanza 16, line 3); he concludes by offering her some advice – she must learn to 'control herself' ('vlastvovat' soboiu', stanza 16, line12). So goes his 'sermon' ('tak propovedoval', stanza 17, line 1).

Is this an example of Evgenii's nobility, or is this priggish posturing, as the self-pitying and melodramatic 'I was not created for happiness' may suggest?[24] In stanza 13, the narrator suggests that Onegin has behaved well ('milo ostupil', line 2), and offers a diatribe against those who persist in seeing only Onegin's blacker side. This Chapter is a particularly digressive one (as Cizevsky notes, 246), and Tat'iana's broken heart appears forgotten as the narrator (stanzas 19-22) rants about 'friends'. A friend, like one's relatives, will smilingly stab you in the back; the narrator defines relatives as people whom one hypocritically cherishes (a reference here to Onegin's attitude to his uncle, no doubt). No one is to be trusted for loyal support, snorts the narrator, not even a wife; love is a cruel trick, ('liubov'iu shutit satana', stanza 21, line 14). On whom should one depend? Oneself, he suggests (stanza 22). Thus, Onegin's kind action is juxtaposed with a discussion of egoism arising out of disillusionment.

Poor Tat'iana now becomes pale and even more silent. The narrator switches hastily from discussing her to a more positive scene of love. Ol'ga and Lenskii appear to be getting on famously; Pushkin discusses their relations in the Romantic style Lenskii himself would use (Lotman, 243), interspersing his comments with digressions on young lady's albums (in which friends, etc. would write comments; Lenskii, passionate as the minor Romantic poet Nikolai Iazykov, leaves tender verses in Ol'ga's). The narrator contrasts these silly provincial collections with the 'odd tomes' ('razroznennye tomy', stanza 30, line 1), more pretentious albums collected by society ladies, created by serious men of verse, decorated by the artist F.P. Tolstoi, and in which one might find Baratynskii's verses. Another digression deals with the attack on the Russian elegy form made by the poet and liberal thinker Wilhelm Küchelbecker, who in 1824 criticised the Russian elegy for its triteness and vagueness, while praising the ode.

Pushkin only returns to the main subject (allegedly) in stanza 37, when he begins a description of Evgenii's daily routine, interspersed with comments on nature (see Mikhailovna, 51-60). Onegin is now living like an 'anchorite' (stanza 37, line 5). As lightly attired as Byron (i.e. as the creator of Gulnare, the heroine of *Corsair*), he walks, swims the 'Hellespont' (stanza 37, line 10), an ironic likening of the local river to the strait swum by the ardent Leander to reach his love, reads, rides, sleeps, and eats his dinner in solitude. He forgets the passing of time.[25] In stanza 40, however, the narrator reminds him of time by referring to the onset of autumn; November approaches, the frost appears (this is the first of three detailed descriptions of winter in this text; see Nabokov, II. 473). Suddenly there is nothing to do, for the weather keeps one indoors, reading (the political work of Dominique de Pradt, or Sir Walter Scott: Pushkin juxtaposes a prosaic writer with a romantic one) or doing one's accounts – but, at any rate, bored. A Byronic allusion is made: Evgenii, like Byron's Childe Harold, 'gave in to pensive laziness' ('vdalsia v zadumchivuiu len'', stanza 44, line 2), although he also spends some time playing billiards, as the ironic narrator points out. He is even pleased to see Lenskii for the variety this offers; stanzas 45-51 deal with the dinner of which the two 'friends' partake (the narrator has time for a digression on champagne) and with chat about the

Larins; Lenskii persuades Onegin to go to Tat'iana's name-day party on the Saturday. The final two stanzas in the Chapter (stanzas 50-51) describe Lenskii's happiness, for he is shortly to be married to his beloved Ol'ga. Happy is he who is 'devoted to belief' ('predan vere', stanza 51, line 3), who can ignore reason and live drunkenly, passionately, like a butterfly drinking of nectar, says the narrator in stanzas which oppose naive idealism to scepticism, poetry to prose (Lotman, 256).

Chapter V: Divination, dream, and potential disaster

The epigraph that sets the scene for this chapter is taken from *Svetlana* (1812), a poem to which Pushkin has already referred in Chapter III (when Lenskii called Tat'iana 'silent and sad as Svetlana'), and to which he will refer again in stanza 10 of Chapter V. The lines chosen for the epigraph come from the ballad's *Epilogue*: 'O, know not such terrible dreams, you, my Svetlana!', and introduce both the focus of the action of Chapter V, Tat'iana's terrible dream, described in stanzas 11-21, and the theme, which is that by now familiar one of the relationship between dreams and reality. Another important event is Tat'iana's name-day party.

Pushkin introduces the allusion to *Svetlana* for purposes of ironic contrast. Svetlana's dream of foreboding is countermanded by the happy ending which takes place after she wakes; Tat'iana's dreadful dream, however, does come true. Zhukovskii's heroine dreams that her lover carries her off, not to happiness, but to show her his grave; Pushkin's Tat'iana is carried off by a bear, and finds herself at a terrible feast of monsters, during which Onegin and Lenskii fight, and Lenskii falls, presumably dead. Svetlana wakes from her dream of death to an artificially romantic reality which permits her marriage and happiness; Tat'iana wakes to a reality which, later, will encompass Lenskii's death and her own unhappiness. Her dream is a true portent of destruction, signifying not only the death of Lenskii, but of love in general.[26] Pushkin, in this most 'literary' of novels, suggests that life, with its 'everyday and psychological realism' (Lotman, p. 258), does not imitate art. Onto this ironic parallelism, Pushkin grafts a mystery: do dreams come true? Whether or not Pushkin himself was superstitious (as Cizevsky claims, p. 257), foreshadowing is certainly a clever device in this textual 'game' that Pushkin plays with his characters' lives, which constantly move between the real and the artificial, and now which move between the real and the supernatural as well – as the author ponders what 'reality' is.

Pushkin starts with a description of the seasonal transition from autumn to winter as the year of 1821 begins, carrying connotations of fresh hope as the world is transformed into bright and clean white. In stanzas 2-3 Pushkin inserts a cynical undertone to this lyrical depiction of nature, parodying the florid verse of Viazemskii and Baratynskii, and introducing overtly sentimental images of fluffy ('pushistyi') snowdrifts (Pushkin uses the Church Slavonic 'brazdy', a sonorous word which makes the accompanying epithet 'pushistyi' seem even more inappropriate) and a boy dragging a dog (a 'pooch', as Nabokov rather nicely translates it; Johnston has 'pup', for 'zhuchka') about on a sled. The year is a new one, but the future cannot come quickly enough for impatient girls; stanza 4 introduces the theme of foretelling by discussing ritualistic activities which traditionally take place on the evening of January 5th ('Kreshchenskii vecher', or Epiphany Eve), the time for guessing fortunes. Tat'iana, whose superstitious nature Pushkin describes in stanza 5, enjoys such games, and even the fear that ominous portents inspire, and believes fully in the efficacy of such activities as melting wax and then placing it into water, so that it forms portentous shapes, or of directing her mirror at the moon in the hope that her husband-to-be's face will be revealed.

In a scene which has established Tat'iana for many critics as an essentially 'Russian' soul (undeservedly so, in the opinion of other critics, who point out that Tat'iana is a lover of foreign novels, and expresses her deepest emotions not in Russian, but in French), Pushkin describes the drawing of trinkets at random from a covered dish of water. While this takes place, he offers snatches from dish-divination songs which span the opposing themes both of death and marriage, a dualism which the *Svetlana* ballad incorporates and resolves for the better, but which Pushkin's poem reveals as an ironic opposition. Death, rather than marriage will be the result of tempting fate to reveal itself. Even if not death, disappointment may well be the result, as Pushkin suggests when he describes the ritual of accosting the first person to pass the gate, who allegedly bears the name of one's future spouse; Pushkin imagines her hearing the old-fashioned and rather amusing name 'Agafon', hardly the name of the romantic hero of which young girls dream.

Tat'iana balks at the dangerous act of setting a table for two in the bathhouse, a ritual which may conjure up the presence of a spirit who may possess the knowledge she seeks, but goes to bed with the pagan god of love, Lel', in her thoughts, and a looking-glass under her pillow, ready to receive the beloved image she hopes will appear. Her dream, a 'chudnyi', or marvellous dream indeed, begins with Tat'iana on a snowy, dark plain intersected by a swollen river which has overflowed its banks and across which a flimsy bridge provides the only way forward – until a bear appears out of a snowdrift and offers a helpful paw, albeit one with 'sharp claws' (stanza 12). The bear, who possibly represents Tat'iana's husband-to-be, pursues an increasingly terrified Tat'iana, who flees into a wood, where branches hamper her progress, and where she loses shoe and scarf, until, ultimately, she falls down (stanza 14). The bear carries her to a hut where his friend is to be found (Pushkin uses the word 'kum', but to suggest cousinship, rather than in its precise meaning, of 'godfather'; Onegin is related to Tat'iana's husband, as we discover in chapter 8, stanza 18). Tat'iana, peering into the next room, where she can hear sounds as if of a wake (stanza 16), sees a strange company gathered round the table.[27] Pushkin's listing of a horned creature with a canine face, another with a cockerel's head, a witch with a goat's beard, a skeleton, a dwarf, and something half-crane and half-cat, a crab on a spider's back, a goose with a skull for a head, and a dancing windmill, culminates with reference to the fact that Onegin is present, and, as we learn (stanza 18), is the host at this strange gathering.

Onegin is presented as an ambivalent figure; both a man at home with a party of monsters, and yet Tat'iana's 'hero', who, when the monsters, on seeing Tat'iana, clamour to own her, with shouts of 'mine, mine' (stanza 19), asserts his ownership, seats her on a bench and lays his head on her shoulder. Does Tat'iana see Onegin, her 'Grandison', as a monster who can be tamed by love? The reader might be forgiven for scepticism, for immediately Ol'ga and Lenskii enter and Onegin flies into a rage at being disturbed. The animal resurfaces in him as he seizes a knife; Lenskii is thrown down; and Tat'iana wakes at this fateful moment (stanza 21, line 6) to discover that it is dawn, and Ol'ga is entering to question her on whom she saw in her dream. Both husband and beloved, presumably, although Tat'iana – who turns to a book by the foreteller Martin Zadeka (see Nabokov, II, 514-6, or Brodskii, pp. 131-2 on the identity of Zadeka) for an interpretation – understands only that some dire event seems likely to occur.

Tat'iana's name-day, January 12th, is now the focus of the narrative. Pushkin details the bustle of the arriving guests in stanzas 25-8, singling out such excellent examples of country society as Mr. Trifle (the fat Pustiakov), Mr. Bash (Gvozdin), the Beast family (the Skotininy), the dandy Cockerel (Petushkov), Mr. Brawler (Buianov, a name probably taken from a satire by Pushkin's uncle), Mr. Flan (Flianov), the so-called 'wit' Triquet, Mr. Throttle (Kharlikov), and an army major on whom the young ladies have their sights. The feast (which bears witness to the Larin family's comparative poverty, for the guests drink sparkling wine instead of champagne, and eat blancmange, considered rather an ordinary dish) commences. The reader inevitably draws a comparison between this gathering and the equally noisy party presided over by Onegin, who now enters, late, with Lenskii, and is seated opposite poor Tat'iana, who must struggle desperately to overcome her emotion. This is a significant moment; can Onegin be moved to pity, as he appears to be later (stanza 34), or even to love? His reaction is one of anger. A combination of a sense of his own lack (for he cannot return Tat'iana's feelings), and irritation caused by his awareness that the guests are observing the two of them (as Brodskii suggests from an examination of a variant of stanza 30 [Brodskii, p. 134, also noted by Cizevsky, p. 262]) impels Onegin to rashness.

He resolves to provoke (Pushkin uses the verb 'vzbesit'', with its connotations of devilish rage, in stanza 31, line 10) Lenskii in revenge for having dragged him into this situation. The stimulus to pity provokes rage and callous behaviour, which manifests itself later when the greedy feasting of the guests is over, including the drinking of champagne from slim goblets (which gives Pushkin an opportunity to make an in-joke in stanza 32, referring to one not-so-slim Zizi Vul'f, with whom he conducted an affair in 1829.[28]

The guests swarm out of the dining-room to indulge in card-playing and dancing until tea will be brought in; Pushkin interpolates an aside in stanza 36, discussing his poetic interest in the theme of food and drink, and likening his depictions to those of Homer. This mock-heroic irony, for these feasters are no heroes, both hints at the 'war' which is to come between Onegin and Lenskii, and reminds the reader yet again of the discrepancy between the ideal and the actual. Stanzas 37-8, which Pushkin omitted in the complete edition because of the appearance of the name of Dunia Istomina, the dancer to whom he has already referred in Chapter I, stanza 20, continue the mock-Homeric mode, as Pushkin compares Tat'iana favourably with Helen of Troy (it is Ol'ga, however, who is to be battled over by these Russian analogues of Paris and Menelaus). Pushkin underlines again the difference between the great Trojan war, fought for love of one woman, and the forthcoming duel which will be fought with love on one side and supreme indifference on the other. Onegin once again breaks himself free of the heroic mould in which he is constantly cast by Tat'iana by acting not out of passion, but out of petulant rage and ennui.

Pushkin describes in stanzas 41-3 the ball (thus fulfilling the promise he made to the reader in Chapter I), which becomes wilder and wilder, suggesting again a link with Onegin's party (which had included a dancing windmill) as depicted in Tat'iana's dream. Onegin dances continuously with Ol'ga, and the situation reaches its climax when Ol'ga refuses to dance with Lenskii as she is promised to his friend; Lenskii leaves, thinking direly of duels. The fifth chapter has established that romance will have its way for the moment, and the quintessentially Romantic image of two men duelling for the hand of a fair lady will be painted in the next chapter; Pushkin has firmly established, however, the subtext to this pretty scene. The bestial emotions felt, such as possessiveness, revenge, greed, and Onegin's desire to kill feeling in himself (a desire which fulfils itself in the rejection of Tat'iana and the slaying of Lenskii), ensure that underneath the bravery and drama lies a grim reality which will now be forcibly presented to the reader during the duel scene. It should be remembered that duel scenes were an essential plot ingredient not only of Romantic literature but of 'svetskie povesti', tales popular from the 1830s onwards in which romantic interludes were combined with a most unromantic social criticisim and a cynical exploration of man's cruelty towards others.

Chapter VI: The duel

The chapter opens with a quotation from Petrarch's *In vita di Laura* (with line 2 of the original omitted): 'There, beneath days misty and brief, a race is born to whom dying is not painful'. Lenskii's death, however, should be painful – to him, to Onegin, who at last realises the consequences of his rejection of pity, and to the reader (Lotman sees the lines as referring to Onegin, whose ennui makes him fearless, p. 286). This chapter is a marvellously skilful interweaving of clichés commonly found in Romantic and Sentimental literature (clichés which distance the reader from genuine feeling), and moments of true sorrow, when Onegin discovers the reality of the painful consequences of grand gestures inspired by Lenskii's posturing and by Onegin's rather Byronic disaffection.

Pushkin begins by describing the aftermath of the ball; Onegin goes home, satisfied with his revenge upon Lenskii, Ol′ga to sleep, and Tat′iana to stand by the window staring into the darkness and thinking of Onegin and his odd behaviour. 'I'll perish', she says aloud, 'but destruction at his hands would be kind' ('gibel′ ot nego liubezna', stanza 3), an oxymoronic statement which sums up the contradictions in Tat′iana's own nature; her tenderness and desire to be treated gently, and yet her love of portents, her enjoyment of her own superstitious fear, her ability to write boldly to Onegin confessing her love. Pushkin moves to a brief description of one Zaretskii, a man with a colourful past, a noted shot, who has now become a model of bucolic stability, like Homer engrossed in the pleasures of country life (see Brodskii on the likeness of this character to F.P. Tolstoi, pp. 137-8). Pushkin introduces a theme which will be developed later in the chapter; that of the dashing and romantic figure transformed into a mundane person, who has at last 'found shelter from storms' (stanza 7).

Zaretskii hands Onegin Lenskii's challenge and receives his curt response – 'always ready'. Onegin is, however, rather dissatisfied with himself, realising that he should not have poked fun at 'love timid and tender' or encouraged Lenskii's violent and youthful feelings; he should have shown more sensitivity instead of 'bristling like a beast' (stanza 11), a line which reminds the reader of Onegin's behaviour in the previous chapter. Such sentiments are, unfortunately, tossed aside as Onegin thinks of his reputation, were he to back down. Pushkin picks up on the seminal theme of the dangerous influence of society, a theme emphasised by the reference in stanza 11 to Aleksandr Griboedov's social satire *Gore ot uma* (1824; published only in 1833 in a censored version). Further references to Griboedov's work are to found in the last stanza of this chapter (46), as well as in Chapters VII and VIII, underlining the similarity between Griboedov's and Pushkin's depictions of a social world filled with empty triviality. It is not surprising that Onegin has been called a consummate 'society tale', a genre which developed in the 30s as an uneasy hybrid of Romantic pastiche and social criticism.

The time and place for the duel are set – the next day before dawn at the mill – and all appears destined to run its course, although Pushkin interlaces into the narrative moments which defuse the dramatic tension of the situation and suggest that the entire matter could be resolved. In stanza 13, for example, Lenskii goes to see Ol'ga only to discover that she is completely unchanged, and that he is still loved. Unwilling to accept the logical deduction, that there is no reason for his jealousy of Onegin, Lenskii cannot relinquish his martyred posturing, preferring to see himself as the saviour of this fragile flower of womanhood from the despoiler Onegin; his high-flown rhetoric is nicely defused by Pushkin, who sums up the situation baldly in the last line of stanza 17; Lenskii 'has a duel with a pal' ('priatel''). Lenskii, unaware of how ridiculous the situation is, goes home and tries to read Schiller (an appropriately Romantic poet), then begins to write verse, which Pushkin 'replicates' for the reader in stanzas 21-22. Filled with clichés and couched in gloomy terms, they amount to a welcoming of death and fate; 'the law of fate is right', Lenskii writes sententiously. Such dark and vague writing is typically Romantic, Pushkin reminds us, though, he adds, he sees no romanticism in it (stanza 23), a hint both at the artificial treatment of themes by self-indulgent sentimentalists, and, possibly, at the idea that there is little that is noble and idealistic in dying over a misunderstanding with a friend who has created a situation merely out of pique.

Onegin, indeed, does not live up to Lenskii's romantic expectations, for he oversleeps and arrives late at the appointed place, and with his French valet, Guillot, whose acting as Onegin's second justifiably annoys Zaretskii. Pushkin asks whether it is still not too late for a reconciliation, but again that fear of social shame spurs on the two friends. In a wonderfully onomatopoeic stanza (29), Pushkin describes the preparations – the loading and priming of pistols, the pacing-off of the distance (32 paces). Lenskii and Onegin start towards each other; Onegin fires after nine paces, and Lenskii falls.

Pushkin surrounds the poet's fall with clichés common to Romantic and Sentimental literature: the sun has been eclipsed by cold (a reminder of the 'ice and flame' imagery used to describe the two friends in chapter 2), the storm has blown itself out, the bloom has withered, the altar flame gone out. In the next stanza (32) he switches abruptly to a more sincere tone, using the image of a deserted house to describe the dead poet. Onegin gradually begins to realise what he has done; Pushkin interpolates two stanzas in which he points out that it is pleasant to kill by wit, but not quite so pleasant to kill in actuality. The point of greatest awareness is reached when Onegin is told that Lenskii is dead (35); but he walks away – his usual reaction being to reject rather than confront deep feelings.

Pushkin now addresses his readers, who, he says in stanza 36, are no doubt sorry for the dead poet, sorry for the loss of his talent, of such fire and feeling, of his dreams (though whether the reader is in fact sorry is a moot point; see Brodskii, p. 143, who argues that Pushkin intended the reader to feel detached from this 'caricatured' character). Perhaps he could have been a great poet?, asks Pushkin, in a tone which can be interpreted as serious or ironic. The tone is more likely one of gentle mockery, for as Pushkin suggests in stanza 40 (the previous stanza is lost), perhaps Lenskii would have lost his youthful ardour, and, as one marvellous line describes it, 'drunk, eaten, got bored, grown fat and sickly' (stanza 39, line 11) and would then have died in any case. Has Lenskii's short but Romantic life been better than a longer and more mundane existence?

Whatever the answer to this question, the narrator is uncharacteristically glum, telling the reader that he cannot continue with the story of Onegin just yet; firstly, he must lament the passing of his own youth and gaiety. Soon he will be thirty (Pushkin himself was 28 at the time of writing these lines). He will now start along a new path, he tells the reader in stanza 45. The final stanza offers his parting words to a bygone era of passions, dreams and indolence, of poetry and inspiration; the poet Lenskii becomes a universal symbol for romantic youth. The final lines develop the image of days 'flowing' which appears in line 2; the flood of feeling has now turned into an 'omut', a word which can mean either whirlpool or deep place in a river, presumably the latter, since the author refers to himself now bathing in that place with his friends, in two lines taken from *Gore ot uma*. Griboedov used the lines to describe immersion in an empty social life; Pushkin refers to his heart 'petrifying in the deadening intoxication of the world', suggesting how the passions become replaced by an artificial intoxication created by the trivial distractions of society. Pushkin again criticises a society in which it is considered bad form to refuse a challenge. The theme of the discrepancy between real feeling, such as the friendship which Lenskii and Onegin have for each other, and an artificial feeling of honour (or fear for one's reputation), is nicely summed up; the one is real, the other a 'deadening intoxication' – a drug which poisons.

Chapter VII: To Moscow

The epigraphs to chapter VII, dedicated to Moscow, reiterate the theme of town and country which has been suggested in Chapters I and II, which juxtaposed Evgenii's city social whirl with rural life on the Larins' estate. In stanzas 4-6, Pushkin describes how the reader, and other 'friends' – those who are intrinsically country people – are called by spring from the town into the vernal countryside. These 'Priams' with large families (indicative of their 'rural' fecundity, one assumes), or those interested in the agricultural writings of Levshin, or sentimental ladies, must rush to the warmth and 'seductive nights' of the country. Pushkin, in his customary ironic manner, juxtaposes reality (large families and farming) with the amatory evenings anticipated by young ladies of sentimental disposition. The narrator himself is torn between admiration of the spring, and sorrow at his own age and autumn years, suggesting again that discrepancy between expectation and reality which is to reach its culmination in Tat′iana's understanding that her heart's desire is available; this takes place in the city, the place of cynicism, rather than in the romantic countryside, where her love has actually been rejected.

In calling the reader to the countryside, Pushkin calls him to Lenskii's grave, now abandoned and forgotten, the path leading to it overgrown. Ol′ga has rather swiftly attached her affections to a cavalry officer, and married him; Pushkin cynically inserts a stanza suggesting that the dead are usually only remembered by those squabbling over their inheritance (stanza 11). Tat′iana is now alone, her heart torn by her love for Onegin, whom she feels she should hate as Lenskii's 'murderer' ('ubiitsa'). She walks abstractedly through the country by moonlight and finds herself at Onegin's house. The housekeeper Anisia shows her round; Pushkin mentions two particular details, Byron's portrait and a bust of Napoleon, which are to be found in Onegin's study. Other details, of billiard-cue and riding-crop, suggest both frivolity and the streak of cruelty which are so fatally combined in Onegin's nature.

The reference to Byron is repeated; Tat′iana is granted permission to return in order to avail herself of Onegin's library, and in stanzas 21-23 she immerses herself in several works in which 'the epoch and contemporary man are well reflected'. These are Byron's *Giaour* and his *Don Juan*, in addition to '2 or 3 novels', the names of which can only be guessed at, although one very likely candidate is Benjamin Constant's *Adolphe* (1816), the hero of which is an alienated and paradoxical type rather like Onegin. *Giaour* (1813), about the love of the Turkish slave Leila for a *giaour*, or non-Muslim, is a tale of hopeless love (Leila is thrown into the sea by her owner) and of revenge, for her lover avenges her. *Don Juan* (1819-24) is quite a different story, a satirical look at sensual adventuring, and one which moreover contains a possible parody of the situation described in *The Giaour*; in Byron's later poem, Juan ends up as a slave to a Turkish princess.

From her perusal of these texts, which bear the imprint of Onegin's pencil in brief words, crosses, or question-marks, Tat′iana begins, she believes, to gain some insight into Onegin's character, which is formed of extremes and paradoxes; he is 'a sad and dangerous eccentric', both angel and devil. These Romantic ideas however lead to a further idea – is Onegin not simply a 'parody' (stanza 24, line 14), i.e. a Byronic imitation? Is he a 'Muscovite Harold' ('Moskvich v Garol′dovom plashche', stanza 24, line 11), referring to the melancholy and alienated hero of Byron's *Childe Harold*, 1812-18), or a collection of 'modish words' ('Slov modnykh polnyi leksikon?', stanza 24, line 13)? Does Tat'iana or Pushkin voice these thoughts? Despite Brodskii's affirmation that it cannot be the latter, it is hardly likely to be Tat'iana, and these statements can be taken as Pushkin's comment on his hero's lack of identity. Both his hero and his heroine, like Lenskii, have formed their lives on literature, and as a consequence cannot be loved, cannot love and cannot live.

What, however, is Onegin to Tat'iana? A vengeful lover, a brooding Childe Harold, an adventurous Don Juan? The Byronic references encapsulate his complexity and suggest that although Tat'iana might not have 'resolved the riddle' of his nature, which is as all-encompassing, presumably, as any Romantic text, she has a ready stock of literary clichés with which to describe him. Pushkin's drafts included several 'entries' in which the reader would learn more of Onegin from his own words (see Nabokov, III, 87-94), but the final version omits these, leaving Onegin still an enigma, though possibly now something of an empty one. If so he is a more fitting subject for Tat'iana's love, which, formed by reading, seeks image rather than substance.

It is 1822. Tat'iana's mother has now decided on taking her recalcitrant daughter to Moscow, the 'marriage mart' (stanza 26), despite Tat'iana's great reluctance to present her provincial self to the mockery of the town smarts. Well might she say that she is exchanging her beloved countryside for 'the noise of glittering vanities', as Pushkin describes it ('shum blistatel'nykh suet', stanza 28). Despite her dread, the fateful day comes in winter (they leave at the end of January; see Lotman, p, 21), and they set off on a week-long trip, for as Pushkin remarks, her mother, travelling on the cheap, uses only her own horses, slowing down the pace somewhat; no 'Automedons' (Pushkin refers to Achilles' swift charioteer) for her. In stanza 36 Moscow is entered: Pushkin greets the city with pleasure in stanzas 36-38. The Napoleonic theme reappears, as Pushkin reminds the reader that Moscow burned rather than submit to the would-be conqueror; he refers to the Petrovskii castle, where Napoleon stayed on September 4, 1812, as the Kremlin was burning. This provides another portent of the novel's ending, for Tat'iana will also not submit to the 'Napoleonic' Onegin.

The Larins are staying with an old and consumptive aunt (stanza 40) of Tat'iana's, who lives in St. Khariton alley in an upper-class district in the east part of Moscow (where Pushkin himself once lived). The Romantic theme enters again as the aunt begins to gossip about 'Grandison', i.e. Madame Larin's old beau, a conversational beginning which contrasts sharply with her lamentation on her own old age, followed by tears, and consumptive coughing (stanza 42).

Tat'iana is taken to visit numerous relatives; her cousins take this newly arrived, 'rather pale and thin', provincial relative under their wings, but

Tat′iana is confused and bewildered. She finds the drawing-room conversation disconnected and vulgar ('Takoi bessviaznyi, poshlyi vzdor', stanza 48, line 4). All is dull, languid and unamusing in this 'sterile aridity of speeches, interrogations, gossip, and news' ('V besplodnoi sukhosti rechei,/ Rassprosov, spleten i vestei', stanza 48, lines 7-8). Pushkin's digs at the hollow world of high society underscore the epigraphs to this chapter. Although, of the three epigraphs, the first two hail Moscow – Dmitriev's 'Moscow! Russia's favourite daughter!/ Where does one find your equal!' from his 'Osvobozhdenie Moskvy' (1795, stanza 1, line 1) is matched by Baratynskii's 'How can one not love one's native Moscow?', from 'Piry', (1821, stanza 4, line 1) – the third is less adulatory. Taken from act 1, scene 7 of *Gore ot uma*, it details Sof′ia's taunt of Griboedov's cynical hero, Chatskii, with 'attacking Moscow'. Sof′ia asks where things could be 'better'. Chatskii's succinct reply, 'where we are not', indicates his dislike of Moscow society, as well as his restless Byronic desire always to be 'elsewhere.'

Tat′iana is, like Chatskii, unimpressed by the glittering whirl of Moscow's social life. She is, one suspects, unamused by the 'archival youths' (those of upper-class birth who worked in the Moscow Archives Office), although the poet (and friend of Pushkin) Viazemskii finds favour with her (stanza 49). She is largely ignored by the society crowds at musical or theatrical events, or at the ballet; when taken to the Sobranie Club, described as the haunt of marriageable girls, fops and hussars, she sits miserably between two aunts, thinking longingly of the countryside. However, she attracts the attention of a certain 'fat general'; and the reader suspects that her destiny is about to be determined. Despite the criticism that was lavished on this chapter, which Pushkin's contemporaries found banal and uninteresting, Pushkin has achieved his presumed intention admirably; Tat′iana has lost not only Onegin, Lenskii, whom she thought of as her brother-in-law, and Ol′ga, but has lost her beloved countryside as well, and is about to lose her remaining freedom by being married off. The contrast between the second half of this chapter (stanza 27 of the 55, although 3 are missing, contains the fatal decision to go to Moscow) and the first half, in which the narrator waxes lyrical about Lenskii and spring, is marked. Tat′iana's life has been leached of energy and joy since her removal to the city; the verses show this.

Chapter VIII: A romantic ending?

The epigraph comes from Byron's 'Fare Thee Well' (1816): 'Fare thee well/, and if for ever/Still for ever, fare thee well', from his *Poems of Separation,* and sets the tone for the forthcoming meeting between Tat′iana and Onegin; the reader's expectations will be dashed, and a farewell to love, not a celebration of union, will be depicted (see Lotman, 335-6 on other interpretations).

The chapter begins with the narrator speaking of his schooldays at the Lycée in Tsarskoe Selo, where he first began to write poetry, and read Apuleius (author of *The Golden Ass*, an erotic tale about a man transformed into a donkey; Cizevsky suggests that Onegin would not have read the original, but work modelled on its amorous scenes, p. 285). After a stanza and four lines (the remaining 10 lines of stanza 11 are preserved only in manuscript form), in which Pushkin refers to Derzhavin, who visited the Lycée in 1815, the narrator continues, describing his early, passionate life (stanza 3), and his 'fleeing' to the Caucasus. The latter is an appropriately romantic place, associated possibly with Zhukovskii's Svetlana, riding with her dead fiancé (Nabokov, III: 152-3).

In stanza 6 Pushkin tells us that he is taking his Muse for the first time to a 'society party' (a 'svetskii raut'), where she meets – Onegin. A flurry of questions appears as Pushkin wonders how Onegin has come to be here, and what 'role' he will now appear in; will he adopt the guise of an outcast, of a Melmoth (the reference is to Maturin's Romantic novel, *Melmoth the Wanderer*, mentioned in III: 12); will he be a cosmopolitan, a patriot, a Harold (referring to Byron's restless Childe Harold), a Quaker, a bigot, or a good fellow ('dobryi malyi')? This hardly serious list of possibilities allows Pushkin to launch into a dialogue (either with himself, or with his reviewers, as Nabokov argued, or, less likely, with society, as Brodskii suggests) in which he asks why Onegin is so unfavourably judged. Do we judge him by our own mediocrity? asks Pushkin with some acerbity, and launches into stanzas (10 -13) which discuss Onegin's aimlessness, his travelling, until even journeys became tedious to him and he returned to find himself 'like Chatskii' (stanza 13). The Griboedov references culminate in this direct linking of the cynical Onegin to the protagonist of *Gore ot uma*, who returns after a three-year sojourn abroad. Onegin has been away for about three years; it is now August of 1824 (see Nabokov, III, 167), and he left Petersburg on the 3rd of July, 1821 (see Lotman's chronology, p. 22).

Onegin's journey:

off to Odessa...

Pushkin had originally intended to devote an entire chapter (the eighth) to his hero's wanderings. The section was then taken out, and a number of stanzas left incomplete or destroyed, presumably because of the politically dangerous views they contained, deriving from Onegin's observance of aspects of Russian life under tsarist autocracy as he travels about the country. Although the edition of the novel which appeared in 1832 contained only 8 chapters, an additional section appeared in the editions of 1833 and 1837, entitled 'Fragments of Onegin's Journey'. The fragments consist of

18 full stanzas, with a few lines from 3 more (see Cizevsky for the 134 variant stanzas, 296-300).

Onegin travels from Moscow to Nizhnii Novgorod, to Astrakhan, then to the Caucasus, where he meditates on his ennui, which contrasts so oddly with his physical youth and strength. He then moves on to the Tauris, (the Crimea), land of heroic tales such as the legend of Pylades and Orestes, who escaped being sacrificed by King Thoas of Tauris; this is the land where the famed Mithridates, the king of wealthy Pontus, died, and the place which occasioned the *Sonety krymskie* of the Polish poet and patriot Adam Mickiewicz.

Pushkin moves us from the exotic landscape with its dreams and wild seas, to a more prosaic setting; one should forget the romantic landscape of one's past youth, and now other 'pictures' are both 'needful' and 'liked'. Pushkin paints a rather drab Russian scene, complete with ducks and cabbage soup, but filled with peace ('pokoi').

Pushkin, mentioning the rain in the cattle yard, another unaesthetic detail of this drab scene, compares his own words now to the poetry of his *Bakhchisaraiskii fontan*, which he composed while living in Odessa; Onegin, he tells the reader, is now following in Pushkin's footsteps, and 'remembers' Pushkin when he arrives in the area. Pushkin moves into a depiction of the city; Odessa is dusty, hot, shadeless, and muddy during the rainy season, an image which further deflates the attractive vision of the cool fountains of Bakhchisarai; Pushkin takes up the theme of an appreciation of beauty replaced by an awareness of the mundane. All is not completely unappealing, however; Pushkin describes his participation in the sunny and cosmopolitan life of Odessa, noting such pleasant things as the Casino club, the oysters, dinners at Automne's restaurant, the opera, where Pushkin catches sight of a 'merchant's wife', presumably Amalia Riznich, whom he courted (amongst others) during his Odessa period, and where the 'sons of Ausonia', the Italians, sing playful tunes after the performance. These stanzas, with their gay portrait of Italianate Odessa, end abruptly with the line 'And so, I was then living in Odessa'.

...and back to Tat'iana

Onegin's journey, in the fragmented form in which it remains, adds little to our understanding of his development, as it simply underlines the fact that Onegin's restlessness will never be cured; even Odessa is at times a place not of poetry, but of mud and heat. However, Onegin's restless, Byronic pessimism is about to be overturned by Tat'iana. She appears in stanza 14, married, her husband the general with her. What kind of man is the latter? Pushkin leaves the reader to imagine whether he is the man referred to in the previous chapter, the 'fat general', or a comparatively young man (young generals being relatively common after the Napoleonic wars). Is he a man crippled from war wounds, 'maimed' (as stanza 44 later suggests) or simply a man who has been romantically wounded? (It has been argued that Tat'iana's husband is only around the same age as Onegin, i.e., 28, and has merely been wounded several times; see Brodskii, p.178; Slominskii has calculated that Tat'iana's husband is around 32, Slominskii, 1959: 345). What is in no doubt is the fact that Tat'iana herself is a changed woman; calm, controlled, and mature, although the country girl is still to be seen in her quietness and simplicity. Tat'iana, although 'not a beauty', eclipses even that dazzling charmer, Nina Voronskaia (whose prototype amongst the society beauties of Pushkin's day is still not clear). Tat'iana is a 'faithful reproduction du *comme il faut*', i.e. of good taste, remarks Pushkin, suggesting that his heroine is only playing a part, or is another 'imitation', like Onegin himself, who imitates a Byronic hero; neither's true identity has developed. Onegin is intrigued, and asks the general, his kinsman to introduce him; Tat'iana, now the perfect, reserved society dame, betrays no emotion (stanza 18).

Onegin's shock is as great as the reader's. How could the passionate Tat'iana who had written him such a letter have so completely become 'indifferent' ('ravnodushna', stanza 20). Has society corrupted her so absolutely? Onegin goes home in pensive mood, and the next day, when he receives an invitation to Tat'iana's soirée, accepts with alacrity. Can it be that love has stirred within him, asks Pushkin (stanza 21); Onegin is certainly strangely tongue-tied before Tat'iana. Pushkin notes that his heroine has the 'cream' of society at her party, described somewhat jeeringly as consisting of, among others, fools, old women, unsmiling girls, a man whose old-fashioned wit is now deemed ludicrous, a 'cross gentleman', annoyed with everything, and Prolasov, a man fêted for the 'baseness of his soul'. It is Tat'iana, however, who absorbs Onegin's attention. Pushkin interpolates a snide comment on Onegin's desire for what is now 'forbidden fruit'; is it not that Tat'iana, now both indifferent and married, is much more tempting than the girl who offered him her heart (stanza 27)? Perhaps Pushkin's verse also reflects his own interest, at the time of writing the verse, in Annette Olenina, who, however, refused his proposal.

Tat'iana, despite Onegin's passionate paleness and close attentions, appears oblivious, driving our hero ultimately to write her a letter. The ironic parallelism noted by critics is now obvious; he who inspired a devoted missive now offers his own, rather inferior statement. Onegin's letter of 60 lines (inserted between stanzas 32-3), parallels Tat'iana's letter in many ways (see Cizevsky for the exact correspondences, p. 290). The tone is passionate (critics have noted the similarities with Rousseau, *Adolphe,* and, possibly, Richardson) through which Onegin laments that he scorned the one he loved for the sake of 'freedom', substituting liberty and peace for happiness, a mistake for which he has now been punished. The 'cold' Onegin is now aflame with love (Pushkin uses the verb 'pylat'', to blaze) and surrenders himself completely to Tat'iana, who will decide his fate.

The reader's expectations that this appeal might melt the heart of Tat'iana are defeated; there is no reply to his letter, nor to the next two. When they meet at a gathering, her face betrays only wrath ('gnev') and, perhaps, the fear of scandal (stanza 34). Onegin, in despair, hides himself away and begins a frenzy of reading. Pushkin lists ten authors ranging from the historian Gibbon to more Romantic works by Rousseau, de Stäel and Manzoni, in addition to works of philosophical and medical 'guidance', which may help him to understand his passion and despair, by Chamfort, Fontenelle, Bichat and Tissot. He reads the current journals as well, allowing Pushkin to add a comment on the moralistic tone of much of the literature of his day, and the abuse frequently heaped upon him by critics (stanza 35). The importance of the theme of reading in the text has now been developed significantly, as the Romantic texts which Onegin and Tat'iana both read previously have been supplanted to a degree (in the former's case) by more practical works dealing with the problems of existence.

Onegin loses himself in reverie, falling into such a state that madness, or transformation into a poet must surely await him, as Pushkin snidely informs the reader, describing Onegin humming romantic songs ('Benedetta', and 'Idol mio'). Time passes, however, and Onegin eventually wakes from his 'hibernation' ('on zimoval kak surok', Pushkin states, adapting a French idiom which resonates comically) and goes to see Tat'iana. He finds her alone and in tears, rereading one of his letters (the theme of reading recurs), and falls at her feet (stanza 41).

Yet the great Romantic climax is not to be. Tat'iana eventually asks him to rise and hear her 'urok' (just as she listened to his on that fateful occasion in the garden). She questions his motives; does he pursue her now, she asks, because she is 'bogata i znatna/Chto muzh v srazhen'iakh izuvechen'? (stanza 44) Or does he seek scandal and prestige? Telling that her sophisticated life means nothing to her, Tat'iana bids farewell to the past. It is too late; she is married and, as she tells Onegin, despite her love for him, will 'always be true' to her husband (stanza 47).

Onegin is 'thunderstruck' , but cannot say anything, for Tat'iana's husband comes in. Pushkin then devotes the remaining lines in that stanza (48) and the next three to parting; it is time to leave his Onegin forever. In words which have offered critics much food for thought, Pushkin talks of his 'free novel' ('svobodnyi roman'), and of 'life's novel', the second statement bringing the reader to a consideration, again, of that thin boundary between life and art, which Onegin has in his turn sought to cross, only to be confronted by unpleasant reality, intent on thwarting his desires.

Has the tale really ended here? The existence of Onegin's *Journey*, and of the so-called Tenth Chapter, and the stanzas within it, have provided considerable ammunition for critics, particularly those who would have liked to see

Onegin becoming a Decembrist.[29] Given the unresolved nature of this debate, the 'finality' of either the *Journey* or of the Tenth Chapter can only be regarded hypothetically, and to all intents and purposes, the novel has finished with the lines extolling that he is blest who has not 'lived life to the end', who has not 'drunk the cup to the lees', who has not read life's novel to the end, and can therefore part with it – as the narrator does with Onegin. These final lines send the reader away in pensive mood, and still unsure of what Pushkin means precisely. Pushkin appears to be saying that the ability to part – whether from love, youth, or dreams – is a useful talent to possess. For, ultimately, everything passes.

Notes to Part Two

1. Although not all critics think so. Larry Gregg has some ironic comments to make on Nabokov's work in general, and on his notes to and translation of *Evgenii* in particular, in 'Slava Snabokovu', *Russian Literature Triquarterly* 3 (1972), pp. 313-29. See also A. Dolinin, 'Eugene Onegin', in V. Alexandrov (ed.) *The Garland Companion to Vladimir Nabokov* (New York, Garland, 1995), 117-30, and G. Smith, 'Notes on Prosody', also in Alexandrov, 561-66; see also G. Fenina, 'O nekotorykh aspektakh kommentirovaniia Nabokovym romana A.S. Pushkina "Evgenii Onegin"', *Filologicheskie nauki* 2 (1989), 9-18.

2. See E.J. Simmons's comparison of the first four of the translations listed above, in 'Some English Translations of Eugene Onegin', *Slavonic and East European Review* xvii, no. 49 (1938), pp. 189-208, and J.T. Shaw's 'Translations of Onegin', *Russian Review* 24 (1965), 111-27.

3. French appears to be the best language; compare the two translations below of the final lines of the novel:

Glückselig, wer, solang noch dauert   Das fest des Lebens, es verlat)
Den Klen nicht austrinkt bis zum Rest,   Aufs Ende des Romans nicht lauert
Und Abschied nehmen kann im Nu   Wie ich es von Onegin tu.

Hereux celui qui sut très tôt   Quitter le banquet de la vie
Sans y boire jusqu'à la vie   Sans en lire le dernier mot
Et soudain déclara forfait,   Comme avec Eugène j'ai fait.

The German translation is from Rolf-Dietrich Keil's *Jewgenij Onegin* (Gieen, Wilhelm Schmitz Verlag, 1980) (dual-language text); the second from Maurice Colin's *Eugène Oniéguine* (Paris, Université de Dijon, 1980) (a translation and brief commentary). On other tranlsations, see M. Rosza, 'Die Veranderugen von Onegins Gestalt in den Übersetzungen von Freidrich Bodenstedt und Karoly Berczy', *Studia Slavica*, 38, Nos. 3-4 (1993), 353-64, and E. Markstein, 'Auf der Süche nach dem deutschen Onegin', *Wiener Slawistischer Almanach*, 10 (1982), 137-49.

4. This character was initially called Fadeevna, then Filip'evna, becoming Filat'evna in the 1837 edition. The BCP edition has *Filip'evna.*

5. A woman called Nina Voronskaia is named in the novel, but did not exist – this is merely an imagined name for a typical society belle.

6. Lotman has the best analysis of the chronology of the text (Lotman,

1980: 18-23). See also Shaw (1981), p. 41-2 for further detail on Onegin's life, and Baevskii (1983), 119-20.

7. See Iu. Nishikov's argument that Pushkin and Onegin could not have met in the summer of 1820, for Pushkin was exiled in May of that year. Iu. Nishikov, 'Khudozhestvennoe vremia v "Evgenii Onegine" A.S. Pushkina', *Filologicheskie nauki* 5 (1984), 9-14.

8. For a detailed examination of this epigraph, see S. Bocharov, 'Frantsuzskii epigraf (1991); also S.N. Grombakh, 'Ob epigrafe k "Evgeniiu Oneginu", *Izvestiia ANSSSR. seriia literatury i iazyka* 28 (1969), 200-19.

9. The omitted reference is to the scholar Petr Pletnev, who had assisted Pushkin with the publication of Chapter I.

10. The topic of Russian Romanticism is a far more complex one than my brief description above can show. Readers are recommended to consult *Problems of Russian Romanticism* (ed. R. Reid) (Aldershot/Vermont, Gower, 1986) which contains a useful collection of articles on the subject.

11. The other literary traditions with which Pushkin 'plays' in Onegin are also dominated by the Romantic tradition: for example, the society tale, a genre popular in the 30s and 40s, the conventions of which are clearly established in Pushkin's novel, also developed in response to (and demonstrate an ambivalent attitude towards) Romanticism.

12. Pushkin's interest in the type can be noted particularly in the character of Germann from ('Pikovaia dama', 1833); Germann (a man 'sans moeurs et sans religion', as one of the epigraphs has it) is prepared to invoke the devil in order to gain wealth.

13. At Talon's 'wine of the comet' is drunk. See N.I. Khardzhiev, 'Kratkaia istoriia "vina komety"' for more information.

14. The second chapter was completed in 1826, after much urging by Pletnev who felt that its appearance, when all the copies of the first chapter had not yet been sold, might boost publication (Mikhailova, 32-4).

15. Which Nabokov claims are German poems; the BCP/Duckworth edition has a footnote in which it is argued that these are Russian. Nabokov's claim, given that Lenskii has just returned from Göttingen and from studies which have included German culture, seems more likely. See M. Iskrin, 'Otryvki severnikh poem', *Russkaia rech'*, 3 (1990), 18-20.

16. The lines dealing with the pronunciation of 'n' in the 3rd verse have caused considerable, if surprising, interest among critics. See S.A. Reiser, 'K chteniiu 6-ogo stikha 33-i strofy 2-i glavy "Evgeniia Onegina"', *Filologicheskie nauki* 3 (1974), and Reiser's follow-up, 'Eshche raz o chtenii 6-ogo stikha 33-i strofy 2-i glavy "Evgeniia Onegina"', *Filologicheskie nauki* 2 (1975); also A. I. Moiseev, 'Kak chitalsia 6-i stikh 33-i strofy 2-i glavy Evgeniia Onegina", *Filologicheskie nauki* 2 (1975), and B.A. Vilenchuk, '"Russkii N" sredi abbreviatur "Evgeniia Onegina"', *Russkaia literatura* 2 (1986); see also Baevskii (1990: 55), and Nabokov I, 296.

17. Other instances of traditional observance are referred to; the Larins like round swings (the seat is moved in a circle by a long pole, the muscle power being provided by a young man), and they like *kvas*, the peasant wheat beer (often used as a soup base).

18. See R. Gregg's 'Tat'yana's Two Dreams: The Unwanted Spouse and the Demonic Lover', *Slavonic and East European Review* 48 (1970), 492-505, and W. F. Ryan & F. Wigzell, 'Gullible Girls and Dreadful Dreams. Zhukovskii, Pushkin and Popular Divination', *Slavonic and East European Review*, 70, No. 4 (October, 1992), 647-69.

19. Whom Pushkin apparently considered a dull dolt, see Brodskii, p. 97.

20. Tat'iana reads pre-Byronic works; she discovers Byron in depth later, in Onegin's library; see J. Falen's *Eugene Onegin*, p. 233.

21. See Lotman on nannies, 216-8; Pushkin's own nanny makes an entrance in V: 35.

22. See Lotman on the 'Russian' nature of this 'translation', referring to Bocharov's comment that it is a 'mythical' translation, Bocharov, 1974: 78; Lotman, 1980: 227-31. Baratynskii is mentioned directly by name in Chapter IV, stanza 30.

23. V. Sipovskii, 'Onegin, Lenskii i Tat'iana', in *Pushkin. Zhizn' i tvorchestvo* (Petersburg, 1907), 571-8. See Cizevsky's argument that this is 'no copy' of Julie's letters, 243.

24. See Brodskii, p. 115, on the Byronic link here with *Childe Harold.*

25. Nabokov argues for a paraphrase of Chénier in stanza 38 in the description of Evgenii's activities, II, 462-6.

26. See the article by W.F. Ryan and F.Wigzell, 'Gullible Girls and Dreadful Dreams. Zhukovskii, Pushkin and Popular Divination', *Slavonic and East European Review* 70, No. 4 (October, 1992), 647-69, in which the authors describe Svetlana's methods of divination in terms of their sources. They mention the parodic (and superstitious) intent behind the allusion (i.e. Tat'iana's dream does in fact come true), p. 648.

27. See Maurice Colin's *Eugène Oniéguine*: 'Enfin Pouchkine utilise avec brio la mode alors fort répandue du fantastique. Le pittoresque de ces tableaux ne doit pas nous dissimuler l'absence de toute donneé psychologique nouvelle', p. 206.

28. Pushkin conducted an affair not only with Zizi, but with her sister, her mother, with Zizi's mother's stepdaughter, and niece Anna Kern.

29. See Jakobson on the allusion to the Eastern Poet, Saadi, to be found in the last stanza, an allusion which in his view introduces a Decembrist theme (Jakobson, 1974: 56).

Part Three: Interpretations

Readings of Evgenii Onegin

The following readings have been organised according to an admittedly simplistic but pragmatic separation of the text into its major components, such as plot, narrative structure and characters, genre, language and metaphor (including versification), literary allusions, setting and chronology (chronotopes), and themes. Such an approach will, hopefully, suggest both the elegantly complete nature of each separate aspect of the text, which acts as a different medium for the transmission of the message, as well as the interconnectivity of all these aspects of the text. The ideas developed throughout each section focus on the issues of 'knowledge' in the text (with reliance to a degree on Bocharov's theories on text and gnoseology), and freedom, aimed at leading the reader towards the idea that the text is about incomplete knowledge, impossible freedom, and unattainable harmony. The ideas of Mikhail Bakhtin on the 'carnival' text are arguably of some relevance in understanding this essentially 'frustrated' (if certainly not frustrating) text.

1. The 'unfinished' plot

Pushkin started writing *Onegin* in May of 1823 and completed the work in October, 1831,[1] the final addition being Onegin's letter to Tat'iana (for more information on the genesis of the work, see Nabokov, I, 60-7). *Onegin* (the unfinished 9th and 10th Chapters aside) is about 21,000 words long and has eight cantos, or chapters, with between 40-54 stanzas in each. The principle feature of the work, as Nabokov has noted, may appear to be its symmetry (despite the loss of the tripartite structure adopted in honour of Dante's *Divina Commedia*, Blagoi, 1929: 184), with the story of two defeated passions arranged on either side of the duel scene. However, such order suggests a misleading neatness,[2] in a text which is open or incomplete, since it is not ended neatly with either the marriage or death of the two main characters (Baevskii, 1990: 12), who presumably will continue to exist in a passionate yet unfulfilled state of love and denial. The reworking by Pushkin of his initial 9 chapters into 8, (after his realisation that the original 8th Chapter would never pass censorship), as well as the existence of the fragments of the 10th Chapter, have led to the idea, championed by several critics, that *Onegin* is essentially an 'unfinished' text.

This belief has even occasioned 'continuations' of the work; Razorenov's 1890 extension of the story has, in rather hilariously melodramatic style, Onegin dying of unrequited passion, with poor Tat'iana left to visit the graves of both husband and beloved, until she, too, dies.[3] There is also of course the well-known Chaikovskii opera, *Evgenii Onegin*, premiered in 1878, which offers in some ways a more accessible path into the text, albeit one that stresses the romantic side to the text, rather than its irony.[4]

Other arguments have raged over whether the final lines of the text are the author's farewell at the end of Chapter VIII, or whether the existence of the 'Journey' stanzas means that the novel ends with the (surely rather unsatisfactory) 'Itak, ia zhil togda v Odesse' (as Tynianov and Tarkhova have argued, 1977: 58-61 and 1978: 267).[5] The Tenth Chapter may even be an expurgated section of a more political Eighth Chapter than was realised (D'iakonov, 1963). The question is, however, whether such a desire to know more and 'what happened next' is the inevitable result of Pushkin's creation of an essentially 'writerly' text, which encourages the reader to enter into the gaps left by the author (as the theoretician W. Iser defines it), or the outcome of a frustrated desire to comprehend a novelistic structure distorted by censorship.

The censored Chapter VIII, dealing with Onegin's journey, and the existence of the fragments of the burned Tenth Chapter, have suggested to critics that Pushkin had intended to develop his text by developing his hero's character. Onegin, the 'parody', was to have undergone a process of maturation; his journey around Russia, symbolic of a quest for meaning, would have ended with his conversion to Decembrism. As Nabokov has argued, Pushkin possibly intended to write twelve chapters in all, completing the tripartite structure with which he initially began.[6] This idea, that the novel would be completed by a political section, has a certain appeal to it, given Pushkin's revolutionary sentiments. And yet, as critics have argued, firstly, the novel is 'finished', in that the love story of Tat'iana and Onegin has been brought to a climax (of sorts).[7] Secondly, as John Bayley has argued, the likelihood of Onegin's becoming a Decembrist appears to be 'impossible' (Bayley, 1971: 240-1), given his character.[8] Simon Franklin, summarising the opposing viewpoints on the abrupt end to *Onegin,* notes textual hints as to a 'notional "real" end outside the text' (Franklin, 1984: 374). He argues that Pushkin deliberately created a 'problem' with the ending, ensuring, through the artificiality of introducing Tat'iana's husband to bring the rejection scene to a close, that 'a sense of natural closure' is avoided (Franklin, 1984: 375). Franklin finds such parody of a natural ending quite in keeping with Pushkin's pastime of confounding the expectations of his reader. As Lotman himself was later to suggest, Pushkin may have avoided an ending to his work not purely through motives of playfulness, but through a desire to avoid the textual 'death' that closure implies (Lotman: 1993: 1).[9]

The notion of climax offers some clues to solving this dilemma of the 'unfinished' plot. The novel appears deliberately intended to be anti-climactic and anti-culminatory; its ending offers the reader the unsatisfactory yet realistic non-conclusion that nothing has been resolved, no happy ending achieved, no passion consummated or grand Romantic destiny fulfilled, no synthesis achieved. In fact, Pushkin's use of parody ensures that the plot is 'deflated', its passion defused, at three significant points in the texts; during Onegin's rejection of Tat'iana, after the duel scene, and during Tat'iana's rejection of Onegin. At each point Onegin and Tat'iana fail not only to achieve their heart's desire, but, more importantly, to gain knowledge.

There are four types of 'knowledge' which Pushkin appears to be sketching in *Onegin*. There is knowledge of the heart, i.e. emotional understanding, and there is conventional wisdom, whether gleaned from books which dictate the rules of Romantic behaviour, or from social mores (see Todd, 1986, on cultural conventions in the novel). A third possible form of knowledge is suggested in the synthesis of the two, in terms both of the match of outward convention with inner feelings, and of the tempering of emotion with honesty and self-discipline; a fourth type is gained through ritual. The three 'climaxes' of the text – the first rejection, the dual and the second rejection – do not provide lasting epiphanies, but a continuation of the collision of conventionality and emotion, with no possibility of a marriage between the two.

During the first rejection, Onegin as the voice of 'good sense' contrasts markedly with the palpitating Tat'iana, but it is easily argued that there is little real wisdom demonstrated in his 'sermon' to her, merely conventional posturing. The dual scene also demonstrates this clash; Onegin is motivated partly by concern for what society might think if he backs down, and partly out of irritation with his own feelings for Tat'iana, which lead him to a violent reaffirmation of his *persona* as a man incapable of friendship (for Lenskii) or lasting love (for Tat'iana). After the duel, Onegin begins to feel and to realise what he has done, and both feeling and insight permeate conventionality. But not for long.

It is particularly surprising that in summations of the plot, the duel scene is usually given little attention; the love story takes precedence (an oversight which Briggs has attempted to redress in his 1992 study). Yet the killing – in cold blood – of a close friend would form the climax of most novels. Pushkin in many ways renders Lenskii's death a non-event; time passes swiftly onwards, Lenskii's fiancée Ol'ga happily goes to the altar, and Tat'iana, her passion for the murderer no whit abated, ensconces herself in Onegin's study. It is her marriage vows which later form the impediment to any relationship with Onegin, not the knowledge of the blood on his hands (which possibly makes him even more of a bold and fascinating figure to her). Feeling is untutored by realisation, and poor Lenskii fades from the text, unmourned. He becomes merely an 'object', i.e. a tombstone (the reification process in the text will be discussed in more detail in section 5).

The third event which provides the characters with the possibility of a lasting synthesis of feeling and wisdom occurs during the final rejection scene. It has been argued that at this point in the plot Tat'iana has 'found herself'; her outward appearance matches her calm inner spirit. This is, however, nonsense, for Tat'iana reacts initially to Onegin with apparent indifference, in utter denial of the emotions raging in her heart. Her rejection of him indicates that synthesis will not occur; that convention (in the figure of Tat'iana) and emotion (now, ironically, represented by Onegin) are still unable to merge. The novel contains an 'unfinished' plot in the sense that its two major characters are 'unfinished' creations, who are still enacting roles; thus Tat'iana's reliance now on the rules of the role of the married society madonna; and her scepticism as to whether Onegin feels real passion for her, or is merely enacting the part of the society rake. Truth has not been found.

As the critics Bakhtin, Lotman, Bocharov and Goscilo have noted, language is put to multiple use in the text, permitting many voices to be heard, none of which necessarily take primacy; there is no single voice of truth which provides the reader with epistemological certainty. As Goscilo has argued, one question that *Onegin* poses is whether language can ever express truth, or only represent multiple possibility and uncertainty (Goscilo, 1990: 284). Bocharov's notion of gnoseology offers the same insight; his argument that in the text there is always a sense of 'translation', that words 'translate reality' (Bocharov, 1974: 75) implies that something is always, of course, lost in translation. Bocharov appears to be using the notion of gnoseology to suggest that man only knows what he 'knows' about reality, not reality itself, and his knowledge is strongly dichotomous (Bocharov, 1974: 66). Pushkin's novel is, after all, only a fragment of that greater whole, the novel of Life (Bocharov, 1974: 103-4). Wholeness cannot be found; man must content himself if he can with a contradictory simulacrum of reality based on subjective worldviews which are constantly fluctuating or 'in transition' as the 'kontrapunkt' created by these opposing images of life is created (Bocharov, 1974: 70). The 'gnoseological structure of reality' is based on 'the relationship of the word to the world' (Bocharov, 1974: 72); gnoseology, therefore, implies many things in respect of Onegin: mystery, fragmentation, dichotomy and falsity.

Of relevance in terms of the sense of incompleteness and fragmentary knowledge created within the novel is the concept of the carnival text, developed by Mikhail Bakhtin primarily in his book on Rabelais.[10] The carnival text, as the term implies, is one of joyful affirmation, iconoclasm, freedom and catharsis; the main characteristic is laughter. Carnival laughter is not merely humour, however; carnival implies unfinishing, undermining all repressive social norms and structures; carnival implies a joyful negation of everything completed or to be completed.[11] It is a kind of existential heteroglossia distinguished by its essential relation to freedom. This is the humour to be glimpsed in the narrative structure of *Evgenii Onegin*, in which difference voices intertwine in counterpoint and counteraction; no voice ever 'concludes' or finishes, but is constantly undermined. No voice knows everything. The carnival text is inherently parodic, for to Bakhtin parody provides a 'corrective of reality', providing new perspectives and undermining closure in any form (whether political, textual or epistemological).

The plot of *Evgenii Onegin*, then, is arguably designed to frustrate any resolution of action. However, the Bakhtinian definition then begins to fall away, for openness implies possibility, and in Onegin, such possibility appears reduced with Tat'iana's rejection of Onegin in Chapter VIII. Pushkin's text is a carnival novel with one apparent and major difference: freedom is both created and denied, as if Pushkin creates both a carnival novel and an anti-carnival novel in one. The very idea of a carnival itself, which suggests catharsis, liberation from established behavioural norms, is relevant to a text in which Tat'iana behaves as a carnival character, forsaking social norms for ritual, or divination (a carnival component) and for openness (as her letter indicates). These are the only 'free' actions in the entire text, and the remainder of the novel is devoted to the at times wistful denial of carnival, while the narrator's jocularity keeps it forever tantalisingly within view. *Onegin* is a cautious carnival.

It could, however, be argued that *Onegin*, despite its limited use of folk traditions and lack of open vulgarity, is very much a carnival text. The novel contains a deep ambivalence towards the concept of (carnival) freedom itself; and ambivalence is a function of carnival. As Bakhtin stated:

> ...carnival laughter is...directed at the highest – at the exchange of power and truths, the changing of world order. Laughter encompasses both ends of the exchange, refers to the process of exchange itself, to the crisis itself. In the act of carnival laughter death and life, negation (mockery) and confirmation (exultant laughter) are combined. This is deeply philosophical and universal laughter. Such is the specific nature of ambivalent carnival laughter.[12]

The plot relies not upon action, nor upon psychological 'action' (for the characters do not develop, and are essentially static), but upon 'narrative action'. Viktor Shklovskii in 1923 pointed out that the plot of *Onegin* is very simple, and should be disregarded; the main content of the novel is its 'own constructive forms' (Shklovskii, 1921: 211). By 'constructive forms', Shklovskii means all the devices which turn the novel into a parody of a love story and which channel the reader's 'willing suspension of disbelief' into a more critical and detached appreciation of the text as an artefact. The plot is of little import; what strikes the reader is the word, the verse; as Tynianov argued, the development of the verbal plane, and the 'dynamic of the word', ('dinamika *slova*') is what develops the action (Tynianov, 1977: 64). The reader's expectations, created through the recognition of an apparently simple plot, are thwarted by the existence of a secondary, 'aesthetic' and essentially narratorial plot which forces the reader to concentrate on the story of the narrator, his thoughts, and authorial actions. The plot remains generically hybrid, neither murder story, nor a plot about character development, nor a story of society, nor, really, a love story, but a plot which cannot be defined, being ostensibly created through actions and yet deformed and undercut by the words. The gap between what the characters actually do, and what is said about them (or what they say) provides a writerly space into which the reader must interpolate his own ideas on how the plot actually works, and how it should end. Plot closure is the task of the reader; it was not the aim of the author.

The plot, it can be argued, once the carnival idea is matched to the concept of frustrated expectations, or desires, functions as a metaphor for impotence, and, therefore, cannot contain climax. The psychoanalytic and feminist approaches taken to the text by Gregg (1970), Clayton (1987) and Rancour-Lafferière (1989) go some way towards this idea, by suggesting that there is a greater sexuality in the text than the majority of critics would allow.[13]

As Clayton has noted, the scene of Tat'iana's dream (dreams being, as any good Freudian knows, fertile ground for sexual imagery) may contain a symbolic 'defloration' of Tat'iana by Onegin.[14] Clayton, however, goes on to interpret this moment in the novel as indicative of a fear of sex (on the part of Tat'iana) which stands also for a fear of death (on the part of Tat'iana's creator, Pushkin). Lafferière alternatively argues that Pushkin identifies with Tat'iana in this scene, and provides some 'clues' as to Pushkin's latent homosexuality in his analysis of the knife in the dream scene, a phallic symbol used on Lenskii rather than on Tat'iana. Onegin either refuses 'masculine' power (when he rejects Tat'iana), or perverts it, as in the dream scene, when he attacks Lenskii, not Tat'iana), with the 'iron phallus', i.e. a knife, which later becomes the gun with which he finally kills Lenskii.

Clayton comes to the interesting conclusion that the dream scene encodes an image of Tat'iana masturbating; his argument contains some useful references to woman taking power into her own hands, as it were. Clayton concludes that Tat'iana eventually rejects Onegin due to his lacking the authority to deflower her when they first meet; 'Onegin cannot offer her a phallus – which is to say that he does not have the authority, or indeed the manhood, to make her happy' (Clayton, 1987: 265). Clayton's ideas can be extended; there is not simply a sexual point to be made from a search for images of phalli and penetration, but a moral one. Not only does Onegin show impotence by rejecting Tat'iana, but he demonstrates it in another way during the 'phallic' scene of the duel, when the aggressive iron of the gun is used on his closest friend, who happens to represent to a degree the emotional, 'female' side against which Onegin strives in his bid to be almost asexual, a hermit. Onegin's progress through the text can be charted as a battle against Woman, in a text which is all foreplay and frustration.

2. The characters

The characters tantalise the reader with their passion, their potential to scale the dramatic heights, but disappoint with their inability to achieve climax. In order for the text to be a carnival novel in the fullest sense of the word, there should be more of a link between bawdy and abstraction, the flesh and the mind, passion and convention, but Pushkin likes to keep these concepts dichotomous. Pushkin's point may well be that the text is 'open' in carnival terms, but not fully 'free', which is another essential component of such a work. *Onegin* is very much a text of freedom curtailed and withdrawn; this 'svobodnyi roman' ('free novel') is no 'novel of freedom'. 'Free' actions, i.e. anti-conventional ones, such as Tat'iana's letter to Onegin, are thwarted; instead of passionate embraces in the *allée* there is withdrawal, separation.

Sexual freedom is denied, unattainable or limited. A look at the context in which references to freedom are made in the text shows the word to be undermined by irony suggestive of freedom's unattainability, from Onegin's first step into 'freedom', when released from the charge of his tutor (I: 4), to Tat'iana's farewell to freedom when she leaves the country for Moscow, to the reference to a 'free novel' in the penultimate stanza of the novel. In Chapter I, freedom (here Pushkin uses the word 'vol'nost'', not 'svoboda', which he uses more commonly in the novel) appears with reference to Rousseau, that famous 'defender of freedom' ('zashchitnik vol'nosti', I: 24) being horrified by a lapse of social etiquette, a moment of minor anarchy, when the French writer M. Grim cleans his nails in front of him. This is hardly freedom on a grand scale. At another point in the text, the narrator asks whether Evgenii is happy, being 'free' to taste of the pleasures of society life (I: 376), and the answer in the negative is expected, for of course Evgenii is merely treading the well-worn path of the young society rake. Should he not try the 'freedom' which is to be found in nature, as the narrator, who, unlike Onegin, is a great lover of the pastoral, suggests? (I: 40). However, nature's freedom might eventually lead to sexual licence, and Evgenii is arguably uncomfortable with that concept.

The theme of freedom's limitations is not purely a linguistic one, although, apart from the lexical references to freedom itself, it is interesting to note how the stanza form reins in the verbal licence of a chatty and digressive narrator. The theme of freedom and restriction is primarily supported through action and imagery. Throughout the text Pushkin constructs scenes which teeter on the edge of licence and carnival freedom, only to be restrained again; the narrator either leaves the scene, or curtails it with a few ironic words, or his characters do. The prime examples of such harnessed carnival instances are the feasting scenes, in which sensuality is given reasonable licence, but which ultimately seem scenes of pseudo-carnival feasting; these will be discussed further in section 5 of this chapter. It appears that Pushkin's characters, although struggling to be free, are doomed to be restrained by conventionality.

The minor characters in *Onegin* do not even have the freedom of rounded characterisation, free from stereotyping, and are treated as caricatures, as is clearly visible during the scene of Tat'iana's name-day party, attended by a variety of stock figures straight out of Gogol. This caricaturisation does impart a carnival flavour – these are 'masked' characters dressed for a farce; however, in this strange society in which all is surface, there is no free and passionate depth, such masks are real.

Certain characters are not even caricatures; Larin, Tat'iana's father, fades from the scene without giving the reader time to learn more of him than that he disliked books, while Onegin's uncle is similarly and summarily dismissed; Tat'iana's husband is a complete enigma (as the debate surrounding his age suggests). Tat'iana's mother Praskovia is more revealing a type; in her youth a devotee of Richardson, yet involved in a loveless marriage, she eventually reconciles herself to her lot, achieves a measure of happiness in her country life, offering herself to the reader as a pattern which her daughter Tat'iana will emulate in her own transition from the role of romantically tragic girl to stoical wife. Ol'ga, Tat'iana's sister, offers an extreme example of this pragmatic adaptability; she leaves the tragedy of Lenskii's death behind her with amazing ease.[15]

The most complex of all the characters is Tat'iana. The central problem for critics, from Belinskii onwards, has been her rejection of Onegin. Is this wrong, or right? Does it show that she has become more mature, or merely more sophisticated? Mirskii has argued that she was 'neither a prig nor a puritan' (Mirskii, 1926: 89), and suggested that her rejection of Onegin indicated Pushkin's own desire to provide his future wife Natal'ia with a pattern of correct behaviour (a rather unusually didactic moment for Pushkin, if true; see Clayton, 1987: 260 on this point; Emerson also has a related comment, 1995: 9). Siniavskii in his controversial 1975 study suggested that she was Pushkin's muse, and so remained with her husband so as to have more 'time to read and read Pushkin and to languish over him'.[16] The paradoxes extend more widely, beyond the issue of her rejection of the man she loves. How deeply does she love? Is she, in the adulatory words of Eikhenval'd, 'the best of heroines, noble in her simplicity, captivating in her warmth of feeling' (Eikhenval'd, 1916: 170), or is she simply a girl with a head stuffed full of romantic nonsense? Is she a parody, as Shklovskii argued? Eikhenval'd himself shows some awareness of the paradoxical nature of this 'warm' person when he likens Tat′iana to Snegurochka, claiming that she is a 'creation of Winter' (Eikhenval′d, 1916: 172). She has been hailed as a typical 'Russian girl', and yet, as critics have quickly pointed out, she writes to Onegin in French, and her reading is entirely Western. Pushkin's manipulation of his heroine's character may derive from a thematic concern with the clash of cultures. Can Russia and the West unite in harmony? A lover of nature, she yet feels alone and unhappy on the family estate, and looks, presumably, to Onegin to rescue her from this. Her behaviour in writing to him is a strange mixture of naivety and daring.[17] A naïve and shy girl, she becomes the epitome of a St. Petersburg *grande dame*.

How is the reader to reconcile these paradoxes, one may ask – but a better question is whether Pushkin intended them to be reconciled. Both Tat′iana and Onegin become the opposite of their initial selves; who could have imagined the wild Tat′iana becoming the epitome of *comme il faut*? Or the bored Onegin panting helplessly at her feet? Briggs sees her as 'not admirable, beautiful, or intelligent, but... utterly charming' (Briggs, 1992: 79); yet, paradoxically, her character includes 'elements of make-believe and inconsistency'; much of her charm is 'spurious' and she is not quite so moral as has been argued (Briggs, 1992: 60). One critic has offered an approach that allows Tat′iana's differences to remain unresolvable, but balanced. Noting that her image is 'in varying degrees derivative, abject, impulsive, passive, majestically disciplined and inexplicably faithful', Emerson admits to 'bewilderment', and argues for an alternative reading (Emerson, 1995: 6-7). Tat′iana cannot be fully understood, for she may be:

> poetic inspiration – which, according to Pushkin's own inspired definition, is neither an ecstatic outpouring of feeling nor a fixed accomplishment but something more intimate, private, disciplined, and creative: a cognitive receptivity of the mind to potentials (Emerson, 1995: 11).

As a creative principle, as Emerson argues, Tat′iana is a form of synaesthesia, i.e. capable of sustaining a large number of balanced dichotomies and heterogeneous impulses, a 'synaesthetic Muse' (Emerson, 1995: 12), or 'dynamic poetic principle' (Emerson 1995: 13). This interpretation is the most satisfying to date of Pushkin's elusive heroine; it can also be developed along slightly different lines. As a 'receptivity to potentials', Tat′iana is to a degree empty rather than creative, an idea which ties Emerson's argument more closely to previous ideas on Tat′iana's parodic or derivative nature as a sentimental heroine. Rather than a poetic source, which retains the imprint of creative potentialities, Tat′iana is a carnival player who swaps one mask for another – taking Onegin's mask which he has discarded as a result of his love for Tat′iana, and denying herself happiness with him in a fulfilling relationship in Chapter VIII.[18]

In Bakhtin's 'carnivals', the image of the mask appears frequently; the mask offers both the object and its distortion in typical carnival transition, as it shifts between object and identity; the mask is 'related to transition, metamorphoses, the violation of natural boundaries' (Bakhtin, *Rabelais,* 1984: 40). The difference in *Onegin* is that such masks are never all taken off at the same time, allowing carnival catharsis and freedom of the self – and sexual liberation. Only in the dream, with its phallic knife imagery, and bestial aspects, does Tat′iana dimly perceive the sexual forces of her subconscious. But she will marry a 'maimed' husband, with all the associations of diminished sexual prowess that implies. She and Onegin will never unmask as carnival king and queen together, before mating.

Onegin's 'mask' is clearly that of Byron's Harold. Onegin is a typical Byronic hero, disillusioned and alienated,[19] a man unable to find his real self, a tragic figure who has always really loved Tat′iana (Eikhenval′d, 1916: 163). But – does he? His rejection of her can be seen as both kind and patronising, as gentle and egoistic.[20] His passion for her later may be only a result of her enhanced social status, as Tat′iana herself appears to believe. Onegin appears fatally driven to postures, firstly as a womanising dandy and young-man-about town, then as a *lishnii chelovek* (superfluous man), driven by ennui and cynicism, and then, secondly as a Romantic duellist (in reality a callous killer), and thirdly as a society courtier. Which role is real, to ask a somewhat paradoxical question. Onegin's tragedy, it has been argued, lies in the disparity between pattern and substance; he is indeed a parody, in the sense of an imitation which exaggerates only the risible aspects of that which is being imitated, but which cannot replicate, or which, in this case, is frightened of, its substance. He can only play at feeling, adopting the guise of the Byronic hero. Thus the paradox noted by Lotman, between Onegin the idealist and the superficial dandy.[21]

As Shklovskii stated, Onegin's fate is 'to be a method' (Shklovskii, 1922: 267). The epigraph to Chapter III, referring to the Narcissus and Echo story, indicates that this may be a text about falling in love with an ideal vision of oneself (Onegin), or becoming an echo of an ideal (Tat′iana); in each case, identity is lost in reflections and echoes. How can the reader know which is the real character? How can the character himself (or herself) know? Another way of approaching this issue is to ask a further question – does Onegin have any clear motivations?[22] From analysis of the events surrounding the duel scene, convention, irritation and a desire to evade feeling collide in his character. He is possibly even jealous of Lenskii, who is so able to show love towards Ol′ga (leaving the issue of whether Lenskii's passion for Ol′ga is real or conventional aside for the moment). Feeling is, for Onegin, something to be avoided, even killed; Lenskii must be eradicated. His flight to Odessa again suggests an emotional withdrawal. Pisarev's 19th-century argument that Onegin is 'nothing' is restated by Clayton, who has argued that Onegin is best defined in terms of what he is not; a non- military, non-functionary, non-Decembrist, non-poet, who is essentially non-Russian as well (Clayton, 1985: 143-5). Onegin is a 'value-destroyer' who stands against the 'value-bringers', i.e. the poets of this world.

Why is he so emotionally stunted? Society may be to blame. Once embarked upon a course of action, Onegin appears unable to break free.[23] Why does Onegin, having forced the duel, not draw back, or fire in the air? His course is set. This argument has some bearing on the view offered by Briggs, who sees Onegin as a particularly individualistic and nonconformist type. Briggs reminds the reader that if Onegin is seen as unconventional, then the rationale given for his agreeing to the duel – that he is concerned with reputation and that 'codes of conduct' rule him – is meaningless. Onegin therefore, 'remains his own man, and what he does must be judged in straightforward terms of moral responsibility' (Briggs, 1993, 60). This reading allows another neat 'cancellation' in the text when Onegin and Tat'iana are brought together in Chapter VIII; his past lack of moral responsibility is opposed by her excess (arguably) of the quality, in respect of her marital fidelity. There is no climax; merely a confrontation of one's self in a different form. Onegin and Tat'iana during the final meeting mirror each other's previous character 'essence': her passion, and his culpability. These echoes from the past prevent real development, synthesis, a moving forward.

The character who forms a trinity with Tat'iana and Onegin should be Lenskii, whose poetic murmurings suggest both conventionality and feeling (he is truly a Romantic in both form and content), and who could possibly form a bridge between the two characters by his friendship with one and his future kinship with the other (he would, had he lived, become Tat'iana's brother-in-law). With his 'Göttingen soul' (II: 6), Lenskii also appears to unite Romanticism (his love of Schiller and Goethe) with an admiration for Kant, whose transcendental philosophy (the primacy of mind over matter) includes a strong rationalism.[24] Yet Pushkin disposes ruthlessly of this inherently cardboard type; as is pointed out, he could have become either a great poet – or perhaps a fat bore. Rather let him die than live to prove the death of love, or its success.

The character who offers 'unity' in the sense that it has been discussed above – i.e. a synthesis of opposites – is not Lenskii, but the narrator, who is arguably the chief character of the work. 'Pushkin' has been referred to as the narrator in the chapter commentaries given above, yet any identification of author and narrative persona is usually rather critically unsound (and renders rather amusingly coy the line in verse 15 of the 10th chapter, where Pushkin refers to the Decembrists reading 'Pushkin's noels'). Critics have argued the idea of the narrator's multi-faceted nature, and his identification or non-identification with the author, back and forth (see Hielscher, 1966, Stepanov, 1974, Lotman, 1977, and Clayton, 1985, 146-9), yet, ultimately, there exists a grey area where all three co-exist, part of the essentially polyphonic nature of the work.

The narrator, a friend of Onegin's, appears to share many of Pushkin's own ideas, likes, and attitudes, yet this is not the primary motivation for arguing that Pushkin himself is the narrator. What seems clear is the intrusive, and essentially authorial nature of the narrative presence, suggesting that the narrator's role is to remind the reader, in a metafictional manner, of the intrinsically literary nature of the text. Rather than acting merely as a narrative vessel, a medium for the furtherance of the plot, the narrator is fairly garrulous (for there is a lot of the 'boltovnia' ['banter'] of which Pushkin wrote in a letter to Bestuzhev in May-June, 1825), digressive,[25] and particularly inclined to converse with the reader on the nature of his own text. He is particularly evocative in his chatter of the style of the social tale ('svetskaia povest'), a genre fashionable in the 1830s and 40s in Russia, and which is distinguished by five types of discourse, all of which are present in *Onegin*. The narrator commands three of these five: gossip, 'moral maxims', and natural conversation.[26] He encapsulates the ambivalence typical of the society tale, which was both iconoclastic, yet conventional (Ayers, 1994: 205-6, Shephard, 1981). His banter is frequently subversive, yet often adopts an aphoristic style, suggesting, possibly, that conversational anarchy may at times yield to the impulse for control and categorisation; the tendency towards the maxim may indeed be 'an inherently conservative impulse' and one which 'gives the speaker a measure of control over the situation' (Ayes, 1994: 38).

The narrator is definitively an author, not merely a commentator, spectator, or friend. In chapter III, for example, he begins to describe Ol'ga, but breaks off, telling the reader 'he'd find her portrait in any novel' and that he himself has 'become bored' with this female character; he does however love Tat'iana ('moia milaia Tat'iana', IV: 24). On other occasions he talks of his 'free novel' ('svobodnyi roman'), or the paradoxes to be found in it, and which he cannot be bothered to repair; or speaks of literature directly in stanzas sparked off by a reference to Lenskii's writing in Ol'ga's album; he is always happy to offer up some 'nonsense' for such books, for he will not – for once – be criticised for his writing; in that same chapter (IV) he refers to a contemporary debate on the ode versus the elegy. Such moments suggest to the reader that *Onegin* is an intentionally artificial construct, rather than a 'story', for in such comments made by the narrator text becomes metatext, suggesting that *Onegin* is indeed a modernist forerunner (Clayton, 1985: 164). The narrator acts as a creative and cognitive presence, undercutting the idea that there are any simple 'truths' to be found in the work, and acting as a carnival presence, deflating, mocking, and always suggesting to the reader that truth is dispersed and unembraceable. The intent behind metafictional constructions is to cast doubt on the author's ability to achieve a truly mimetic creation, and to suggest that the boundaries of art and life interweave; life becomes, therefore, a novel (and a novel, life), as critics have commonly suggested.

The narrator is, as Clayton reminds us, not present merely in the digressions, but also in the tone, in asides, epigraphs and footnotes (Clayton, 1985: 162); his presence permeates the entire text. As Lotman has argued, the artistic, authorial viewpoint is not focussed, but dispersed in varying viewpoints. Lenskii's death provides the most clear example, as it is treated from multiple viewpoints which are at the centre of what Lotman refers to as a suprasystem which is perceived as the illusion of reality.[27] This may lead one to conclude that the 'main unifying factor (in the text) is the I-narrator' (de Haard, 1989: 464). Bocharov, taking Lotman's argument further, discusses the importance of the boundary which separates the authorial context and its 'open diversity' ('otkrytaia raznositel'nost'') from the 'narrow context' of a piece of writing such as that which appears on Lenskii's tomb (VII, stanza 6). The boundary to which Bocharov refers distinguishes 'objective' from 'subjective' writing. Reality, or, rather, its image, he suggests, 'appears in the convergence of two differently-directed stylistic variant ways of expressing it, like their counterpoint' (Bocharov, 1974: 70-71).

The narrator is, therefore, in Bocharov's view, creator of and bridge between two styles, a narrative voice designed to emphasise the subjective nature of reality, particularly as perceived through Romantic eyes. The presence of two styles is furthermore an essential component of the metafictional thrust of the text; it has also been interpreted, as Lidia Ginzburg suggests, as the outcome of a conflict between Pushkin the poet and Pushkin the prose writer (Ginzburg, 1936: 22). This point has been taken up both by Bocharov and by Tarkhova, who argues for the existence of two narrative voices: one reflecting Pushkin-as-man, the other Pushkin-as-creator. Thus, she concludes, the reader hears the voice of the narrative author and the lyrical 'I' of Pushkin himself (Tarkhova, 1978: 9). As Shaw has argued (1981) the narrator develops through various stages, from youthful poetry to mature prose (1981: 35); the theme of the novel may indeed be that of poetic craftsmanship (Fennell, 1973).

Pushkin's narrator fulfils several functions. Firstly, he offers the reader the profit of his wit, helping to turn the text into the 'champagne' effusion it undoubtedly is; secondly, he acts as a carnival, deflationary presence (although, as suggested, he is innately conservative); thirdly, he directs the reader's attention to the artificial nature of the text, and by implication offers a metafictional point, that of ontological relativism and cognitive limitation. His is a presence which is both elusive and disciplined, a static construct constantly yoking the flying fragments of the novel together, returning remorselessly to his plot after airy digressions, but at the same time a presence which fragments and misleads. He suggests that the text is a game, with the reader chasing after the narrator as he runs, weaving many threads through the textual labyrinth. He offers us a whimsical worldview, capable of offering a cynical exposition such as we find in chapter IV, in which the narrator asks to 'be protected from friends' (by whom he appears to mean those who delight in society gossip and mockery); the narrator concludes this section by telling the reader to 'love himself' ('liubite samogo sebia', 4: 22); his only real friend is himself, apparently. Such a 'philosophy' should be judged lightly, however, for this narrator seems unable to take himself, or anything else, seriously. He himself is capable of feeling affection for his characters, particularly for Tat'iana; yet references to love are usually followed by ironic interjections, or even yawns. When meditating on life's transience, he offers the following sardonic couplet, seemingly amused and bored by his own ability to emulate the effusive and rather self-pitying rhetoric of the day: 'Dreams, dreams! Where are your sweetness?/Where, eternally applied rhyme, is youth?', with sweetness and youth providing one familiar example of a clichèd couplet ('Mechty, mechty! Gde vasha sladost'?/ Gde, vechnaia k nei rifma, mladost'?', VI: 44). This is a narrator who has created himself as a parody of an author-poet. He is a carnival author, leading the reader headlong through streets and balls and poses, whose function is to upset, to change, to unsettle and to fill with carnival champagne. But ultimately he leaves the novel with the full 'freedom of the novel' yet to be explored; a carnival narrator whose Bacchic days are over and who now appears strangely passive; an armchair carnival compère.

3. The question of genre

Onegin is, it appears, not a text of action, not a psychological study, but rather, a metafictional novel, as our discussion thus far has suggested. However, such a definition (an anachronistic one, since metafiction is a modernist/ postmodernist concept) implies a certain neatness, whereas Pushkin is clearly anxious to set up genre conventions and ideas only to overturn them. The epigraph to the novel as a whole offers some thoughts on the kind of novel Pushkin was offering his readers: a 'collection of motley chapters' ('sobran'e pestrykh glav', line 10), in the well-known phrase; a novel filled with internal tensions and opposing moods, a text which will not let itself be known, because knowledge means completion and synthesis.

As Pushkin wrote to P.A. Viazemskii on November 4, 1823, he was writing 'not a novel, but a novel in verse – a devilish difference' ('ne roman, a roman v stikhakh – d'iavol'skaia raznitsa').[28] As well as poetic stanzas, which include so-called 'prosaic moments' when the poetic style gives way to a more narrative discourse, *Onegin* contains two letters in verse, a song sung by peasant girls, a poetic dedication of 17 lines, and several epigraphs ranging from poetic quotations to snippets of prose. This is partly what was presumably meant when Pushkin wrote of a free novel; namely, a text which transcends genre boundaries.

The dualism of the text between a prosaic and a poetic style has been analysed by several critics; J. Fennell offered a useful working definition of the prosaic style in 1973, the principles of which he outlined as:

> ...elimination of unnecessary epithets; absence of 'abstract' and vague parts of speech, of periphrases, clichés and hyperbole, etc.; economy of words; simplified syntax with a minimum of subordination; frequent enjambment between lines and quatrains; a tendency to catalogue, particularly concrete objects... To these can be added a considerable lowering of the tone and the introduction of purely conversational elements – both lexical (vulgarisms) and syntactical (ellipses, infinitives expressing inceptive past tense, interjections in place of main verb, frequentative use of perfective verbs, etc.) (Fennell, 1973: 51)

Two worldviews collide in terms of the style of the text; two worldviews are bounded by linguistic conventions, across which the narrator steps.[29] The notion of liminal transgression can be taken as a theme as well, in terms of the social and ethical restrictions with which Pushkin hems in his heroine, leading to her ultimate rejection of Onegin – a rather different situation from her initial, socially daring, action of writing a love-letter to a man she hardly knows in a desperate attempt to escape from her unhappy milieu.[30]

The linguistic format of *Onegin* is therefore a 'free' one, for which Pushkin created his own stanzaic form (see the section below). Form clearly has primacy over content; although the notion of genre is not limited purely to linguistic form, but incorporates notions of thematic and tonal conventionality, as well as the usage of certain iconic traditions, *Onegin,* however, strikes one by its verbal play, its linguistic scintillation. As Bakhtin wrote, *Onegin* differs from all genres, it is 'self-criticism of the literary language of the time' ('samokritika literaturnogo iazyka epokhi', Bakhtin, 1972: 89). Iurii Tynianov, writing in 1921-2, stated that:

> *Evgenii Onegin* was for him (Pushkin) at times a novel, at times an epic poem ('to roman, to poema'); the chapters of the novel turn out to be songs from an epic poem; the novel, which parodies general plot schemes by way of a compositional game ('putem kompozitsionnoi igry'), vacillating, interlaces itself with parodic epic. (Tynianov, 1921-2/1974: 63)

For Tynianov, the novel was an unfinished structure, a combination of novel and verse, in which the verbal dynamics (as Clayton interprets it, the 'banter', or 'boltovnia', Clayton, 1985: 77) is paramount in defining the work (see also Siniavskii on 'banter', 1975: 85-5). How exactly can the 'banter' lead to a definition of genre? The most obvious form of 'banter', the authorial digressions, lead Shklovskii to label the work Sternian, and a parody, the latter idea being supported by the allusive nature of these digressions, which takes one back to the metafictional argument. The text has also been defined as a specifically Byronic parody (Cizevsky, 1953; Stilman, 1958; Hoisington, 1975). 'Banter' also has relevance to another suggested genre definition, that of the text as an extended society tale ('svetskaia povest''). It has been argued that *Onegin* is a consummate example of that genre,[31] containing all relevant aspects (although Belinskii refused to accept that such a genre existed, 1953-9, II: 133), such as unhappy love, a duel, depictions of society, adulterous temptation, a stress on reading (particularly of Romantic literature) and characters who are 'men of the world' (such as the young Onegin), and who appear to '*have no identity other than* as a creation of society'.[32] The text clearly focusses on the social life of the aristocracy, and has as a major theme the conflict between individual and society,[33] yet appears to go beyond the borders of social comment and social depiction.[34] *Onegin* is far more sophisticated an example of a society text than quintessential examples of the genre such as Odoevskii's *Knaizhna Mimi* (1834) and *Kniazhna Zizi* (1839), although in the broadest sense it has the same central idea, namely, that love is always defeated by society. Like the majority of society tales, *Onegin* does not have a happy ending, and love is seen stifled, thwarted, by a society in which passion is seen as far too dangerous to be permitted.

The most interesting approach to a definition of the novel's genre comes from Bocharov, who links the idea of parody to that of subjectivity. A parody, Bocharov suggests, occurs when a literal translation of a 'foreign' subject into the Russian language is made. Whereas Tat'iana eventually becomes the perfect 'Western' society hostess, described in French as 'untranslatable,' Evgenii is a Russian version of a Byronic figure (Bocharov, 1974: 82). Another aspect of the plot has also been suggested by Bocharov, who points to a nesting technique adopted by Pushkin in order to create a metafictional interweaving of art and life. The novel has, therefore, four planes, each linked to the idea of literature; there are 'Tat'iana's novels, Onegin's reading, Pushkin's novel itself, and finally, the 'novel of life', all of which interact to form what Bocharov has called the poetic 'gnoseology' of the novel (Bocharov, 1974: 65).

This idea, which hangs the genre problem on the peg of the notion of polyphony, raises some interesting ideas, one of which is developed by Clayton, who, suggesting that the novel is 'in ironical counterpoint to the expectations of the reader' (Clayton, 1985, 75), argues that the novel exists in two planes. There is the novel as the reader somehow expects it to be, and the actual structure itself, with all its ellipses and fragments. Clayton labels *Onegin* a writerly text (without actually stating this).[35]

The notions of gnoseology, hybridisation, reader expectation, parody and metafiction can to a certain – not to a complete – degree be combined within the concept of the 'carnival text'. *Onegin* can best be understood as a 'free novel' in this concept. Carnival laughter 'frees human consciousness, thought, and imagination for new potentialities' (Bakhtin, 1972: 49). Yet, as already argued, such freedom is waved before characters and reader, only to be withdrawn by the teasing narrator. *Onegin* lacks that true Rabelaisian bawdiness, that focus on 'wine and dung', which permits the definition of the 'body' of the Rabelaisian text as a body open to the world, although the narrator's more sensual digressions do lean in this direction. Yet the narrator only likes parts of the body; his focus is strangely fragmented (as will be discussed in section 5 below). Where it does appear to fit the carnival definition is in its techniques of 'cancelling out', of creating tension rather than synthesis, of epistemological testing, of placing masks on his characters. There are also other elements which belong to the carnival genre (and to its sister genre, the menippea, which is a form of 'weak' carnival), such as sharp changes – oxymorons and contrasts in plot, mood and depiction, the multigeneric elements already noted, topical, journalistic elements,[36] and, perhaps most significantly, a dream which offers arguably one of those 'fantastic situations' which exist, Bakhtin emphasises, solely to test the 'truth' of the hero/heroine's worldview (Bakhtin, 1972: 194). Tat'iana's dream offers her the truth of Onegin's character as well as a chance to look at her own dark desires – that she and Onegin can never love within conventional bounds, but only outside of society. There is no freedom to love within the text. The scenes of feasting are particularly important here; the carnival feast is a temporary transfer to the utopian world (Bakhtin, 1972: 81), and brings people together in a communality; but in Onegin and Tat'iana's world the major feast – that of Tat'iana's name-day party – leads not to union and pleasure, but separation and death. This is what happens when carnival passions and energy are not allowed their natural outlet.

4. The *Onegin* stanza (I:1)

Pushkin's language,[37] with its polyphonic mixture of Romantic cliché, beautiful descriptions, allusions, Church Slavonic, the odd English, Italian, French and Latin phrase or word, switching, contrast, irony, juxtaposition of registers, foreign wordings, allusions, digressions, and humour has already been discussed above in terms of the shift between styles. Other devices not yet mentioned refer to the stanza form itself, such as rhyme, metrics, tabulation, enjambment, as well as those functions of language which exist to provide 'atmosphere', such as onomatopoeia and alliteration. It should be noted (see Briggs, 1992: 12) that this form is deceptively structured, being inherently fluid, thus reinforcing the ideas of convention/freedom so seminal to the novel as a whole. The following section will merely offer some ideas on how the reader might comment on any stanza from the text in terms of the way metre and language produce various effects.

The '*Onegin* stanza', a 14-line form which has some similarities with Italian, Shakespearean or Anacreontic sonnets, or with La Fontaine's rhymed *contes*, but which is definitively Pushkinian, is written in four-foot iambics (8-9 syllable lines) in alternating masculine and feminine rhymes, with the rhyme scheme beginning with a quatrain in an AbAb pattern followed by two couplets (CC, dd), then another quatrain with a different rhyme scheme (EffE) and a final couplet (gg).[38] Exceptions are the 17-line dedication, Tat'iana's 79-line letter, and the girls' song in Chapter III.[39]

There are two differences between conventional 14-line sonnet forms, and Pushkin's. The latter uses a shorter line (iambic tetrameter, or four-foot iambic, versus the usual five-foot, or iambic pentameter), which arguably gives the line more crispness and jauntiness (although there are melodic, drawn-out phrasings). More significantly, the rhyme scheme is also unconventional, with more flexibility after the initial quatrain.[40] Nabokov discusses the verse form in terms of the type of motion within it by using the image of a spinning top, with the opening and closing sections reminding him of the patterns visible when a top spins, while the middle section is blurred.[41] In other words, the stanza advances in the first quatrain, has a variable, or eddying middle in terms of which the two couplets and quatrain (lines 5-12) lose their strict outlines, and concludes in the final couplet (Nabokov, I: 10). In its flexibility, or unconventionality, within an apparently conventional framework, the stanza form echoes the theme already discussed. Pushkin teases the reader with apparent clear forms, while 'losing' the reader within such forms; as Briggs states, two-thirds of his way through the stanza, the reader 'is almost certain to lose his way in formal terms' (Briggs, 1993, ix). An interesting argument is offered by V. Turbin, who likens the 'baroque' *Onegin* stanza form to the floor plan for Witberg's Cathedral of our Saviour (the foundations for which were laid in 1817, in Moscow, on Sparrow Hills), with a mixture of cross-lines, rhymes, and 'circulars' (which represent the cross, parallel lines and circular forms which appear on the floor plan, a diagram of which appears in Pushkin's notebooks, Turbin, 1978: 85-6).

A device which imparts a spurious order is what Nabokov has called the 'tabulation device' (Cizevsky labels it the 'catalogue stanza', 1953: 207), i.e. a listing stanza, such as in the Foreword (Nabokov, II: 24). However, such apparent ordered lists are more than counteracted by the digressions, which allow for a shift within an individual stanza, and by thematic enjambment across stanza (see III: 38-9 for one such example). Nabokov has other ideas such as that of 'overtaking', referring to the sudden speed often needed to shift the scene from stanza to stanza (usually occurring when the digressions have 'delayed' the narrator); in general, the stanzas proceed in first and starts, interspersed with smooth passages, in rather an over-exuberant manner. Overall, the stanza form is intended to tantalise; the rules of the stanza 'game' are there, but the writer does not seem to be playing by them for most of the time.

Taking the very first stanza in the poem (I, 1), the reader can see some of these devices at work (this stanza, with stress marks and divisions into metrical feet, can be found in Cyrillic script in Appendix A):

> "Moi diadia samykh chestnykh pravil
> Kogda ne v shutku zanemog,
> On uvazhat' sebia zastavil
> I luchshe vydumat' ne mog.

The first quatrain begins with a literary allusion to one of Krylov's fables, *Osel i muzhik,* in which the donkey's honest principles lead to disaster for the farmer who hires him.[42] This is a somewhat teasing opening, for who is the person qualifying the word 'uncle' with a possessive 'my'? The reader is left in the dark, a typical start for a text centring on the theme of knowledge. Only later can the reader fill in the details – the 25-year-old Onegin receives a letter from his uncle's steward telling him the man is *in extremis*, and rushes to the estate. This stanza, written by Pushkin on May 9, 1823, is an interesting introduction to the way in which his protagonist thinks; the reader is both amused and slightly scandalised by Onegin's open hypocrisy. The literary range of the novel is also hinted at in this beginning, which is rather a poetic version of the first lines of Maturin's *Melmoth the Wanderer* (a novel referred to again in III: 8): 'In the autumn of 1816, John Melmoth, a student in Trinity College, Dublin, quitted it to attend a dying uncle on whom his hopes for independence chiefly rested'.[43]

The image of death and illness enters the novel in line 2, and is combined with the idea of a 'joke'; Pushkin prefigures the central episode of Lenskii's death, and Onegin's realisation, too late, that this is no joke indeed. The major juxtaposition, or oxymoron, is not that between joke/illness, but the iconoclastic linkage between respect/donkey, suggested by the Krylov allusion and the idea offered in lines 2-3 that now the rich uncle is dying, everyone is filled with respect; how cunning of him – he couldn't have 'thought up' something better. Pushkin brings the first quatrain to a close with the idea that this is all something artificial (as the verb 'vydumat', to fabricate or invent, suggests). The twin ideas of the inability to recognise reality, rather than invention, or to feel compassion for one suffering (dying) – Onegin is concerned solely with profiting from the death – are neatly introduced with a joking tone that creates in the reader's mind a cartoon image of a donkey lying in a human bed, and, in fact, also a carnival, masked image. The iambic tetrameter bounces the lines along breezily, with the masculine ending in line 2 on 'zanemog', echoed in line 4 by 'ne mog' providing two heavy, i.e. less cheerful notes (to the reader only; Evgenii, whose reported speech/thoughts these are, is blithely unconcerned) which in their sound illustrate the uncle's incapacity. The missing unstressed syllable in the first foot of line 3 gives the 'on' more emphasis, a mocking stress, given the context.

The following couplet continues the theme of Onegin's uncle, but very quickly moves onto the subject of Onegin himself in line 2, bored to tears with sitting about waiting for his uncle to die:

> Ego primer drugim nauka;
> No, bozhe moi, kakaia skuka

Uncle is an example to others, says Evgenii facetiously, introducing the idea of learning from a pattern or example which is to influence the behaviour of Onegin and Tat′iana so profoundly. Boredom, that Byronic motif which permeates the texts, is the motif of the second couplet, with the repetition in 'and day and night' dragging the line out tediously, and contrasting nicely with the frustrated rush of the following line, with its image of yearning for escape:

> S bol′nym sidet′ i den′ i noch′
> Ne otkhodia ni shagu proch′!

Onegin is 'fettered', to death, by his own need for the money required to cut a dash in society; Pushkin again underlines the link between death and convention (which are the same thing, it seems, both being anti-freedom, anti-life).

The next quatrain places Onegin in the extremely unbecoming role of carer for the sick, hiding his feelings while he attempts to amuse the sick man, settling his pillows and overseeing the medicine bottle, with the amusing rhyme, 'kovarstvo'/'lekarstvo' making it quite clear that Onegin, this crafty person, would rather be poisoning the old fool. Note the prideful adjective 'nizkoe'; Onegin dislikes such base stooping to flatter (but he does it anyway):

> Kakoe nizkoe kovarstvo
> Poluzhivogo zabavliat′,
> Emu podushki popravliat′,
> Pechal′no podnosit′ lekarstvo,

The quatrain continues the stanza's interweaving of jocularity with an undertone of prosaic, even unpleasant reality, based around medicine and pillows; line 10, with its image of 'amusing' someone 'half-alive' has a macabre tinge to it, and prefigures much of the *carpe diem/momento mori* passages which occur later in the novel.

Literature is again a theme, as there is a link to Byron's *Don Juan*, Canto I, stanza 1 – where Don Juan is referred to as having been sent to the devil somewhat ere his time – hidden in the final couplet:

> Vzdykhat' i dumat' pro sebia:
> Kogda zhe chert voz'met tebia?"

The last line has an emphatic punctuation, with the question mark; this is one minor example of speech emphasis, such as the exclamations, coughs and sighs which impart to other stanzas that quality of orality whence derives much of the sense of spontaneous directness (see III: 38, or IV: 20).

The demonic theme in the novel is understated, and more of a component of the Romanticism which permeates so many of the stanzas, but Onegin is here hinting at the darkness in his soul, arising from his inability to love, to enjoy life, and to regard death, therefore, as anything but a release – in this jocular case, for himself. The reader is, of course, neatly seduced by this irreverent line, and inclined to sympathise with Onegin and the things one 'has to do'; however, irreverence has a way of carrying a moral cost, as Onegin finds out later. As an initial stanza, the mixed tone has been beautifully set for this collection of hybrid verses. Carnival laughter has been created; that type of laughter which contains deep truths, for carnival laughter is, after all 'deeply philosophical and universal laughter' (Bakhtin, 1972: 215).

5. Time, space and images

Although certain events, such as Tat'iana's dream, can be pinpointed with accuracy, time in the text is not completely definable, but is often indistinct and relative (Baevskii, 1983: 123), as are the ages of the protagonists themselves. Critics still argue about the exact dating of certain events, such as Onegin's birth, or the length of time which passes between Lenskii's death and Onegin's return to Moscow, for example.

What forms of time are present in the text? As Makogonenko, who has argued that whereas Tat'iana and Onegin appear to be living 'in the past', the author-poet is living in the present (Makogonenko, 1963: 131), and is still developing dynamically, there may be two temporal layers, or streams, in the text. Nishikov has suggested a third temporal dimension to the text, that of historical progression (Nishikov, 1984: 13), following Belinskii's claim that the text, due to its depiction of Russian society, was historical rather than personal. Other forms of time which are important are the movement from day to night; this is primarily a 'nocturnal novel', in Briggs's view (1992: 38) and from one season to another (Gustafson, 1962). Time is rendered, arguably, deliberately indistinct, so that all the reader is aware of is this very indistinctness, highlighted by the fey moonlight which surrounds that enigmatic moon-girl, Tat'iana. She is associated with the dawn (II: 28) suggesting her freshness and innocence, but the moon quickly takes over (III: 16, 20, 21, 32, VI: 2, and VII: 15, 20), as the temporal symbol of her state (see Briggs, 1992: 38-44 on moon imagery and the 'dark stanzas', V: 5-21). Tat'iana is a shadow who will never be (the reader ignorantly, at first, assumes) part of the 'light' of the social, indoor world. When in the full glare of society, however, she becomes even more opaque. She requires the night – a carnival time – for her full identity to be revealed.

Spatial referents in the text are more clear. There are two main *topoi*: town and country.[44] Onegin moves from his city existence to the country in Chapter I; Tat'iana from the country to the city in Chapter VII. The former implies public life; the country, a more personal and inner life, the life of emotions and the spirit. City life is described in terms of Russia's two main cities (although references to other towns appear in the Journey section). Moscow and St. Petersburg appear in a guise now familiar to readers: Moscow is a symbol of proud Russia, and is also a place of war, as the references to Napoleon and to Petrovskii castle (where Napoleon stayed) suggest; it is also the place of St. Simeon's and St. Khariton's – a place, in short, of history and religious tradition, although Moscow demoiselles appear to spout just as much rubbish as do Petersburg belles, and are equally egotistical, hypocritical, and vain, according to the admittedly rather misogynistic narrator. It is small wonder that to Tat'iana, Moscow is 'stifling' (VII: 53) – particularly the assemblies where young marriageable girls are paraded. Petersburg, in contrast to Moscow's old-fashioned atmosphere, is a locus of hedonistic gaiety and flirtation – of theatres, restaurants, and salons. There is a sense of richness, luxury and sensuality, which at times however evokes a feeling of clutter and claustrophobia. Evgenii's study (which is more like a boudoir), for example, is described in terms of the objects which jostle for space in it – the porcelain, bronzes, amber pipes from Turkey, scissors, combs, brushes, crystal scent bottles (I: 24).

The country, by contrast, is associated with the inner life of the characters and is on the surface of it, suffused with idyllic motifs (Baevskii, 1990: 99); it is also the place of greatest poetic creativity. However, the country is not completely pleasant and pastoral. Nor does it represent freedom, as the narrator would appear to suggest, when he describes Tat'iana bidding farewell to the countryside before she departs for Moscow, and asks also for 'freedom' to forgive her for departing (VII: 28). Within the country *topos*, there are certain secondary spaces, such as the *allée* in which Tat'iana and Onegin meet in the garden of the Larin's estate. This long, fairly narrow space suggests the confining of feeling within convention, as does the idea of a garden ('tamed' nature) *per se*. Tat'iana is shown, initially, when Onegin arrives to respond to her letter, running from the house, the very image of escape, with the verb 'letit'', to fly, repeated to show her haste as she runs to the lake and the grove, breaking lilac boughs ('Kusty siren perelomala') as she goes, as if flinging aside the Romantic conventions symbolised by such flowers (III: 38). She however, ironically, imprisons herself within further Romantic conventions; the image of the young, palpitating girl on a bench by the lake, awaiting her lover, is a typical Romantic trope. Whichever way the characters turn and run in this text, they never seem able to escape.[45]

Tat'iana meets Onegin not amidst wilderness but only after having turned back into the *allée*; and their conversation drags her further back to conventions and restrictions as he hectors her on tempering her passions. Tat'iana shows her unconventionality again when she ventures far beyond the garden, walking to Evgenii's estate (VII: 15), but, as in Chapter II, this is a limited unconventionality or escape for she ends up inside Onegin's house – another image of constriction, particularly with the ghosts of Byron, Napoleon, and Evgenii's dead uncle (all associated with some form of convention) still to be felt in the place.

The house motif is used in other sections of the novel: Tat'iana is shown sitting at the window, tracing Evgenii's initials on the condensed pane as if he will unlock her from her restrictive life (III: 37). She asks for the window to be open before she makes her confession of being in love to her nanny (III: 17), realising that emotion will lead to (carnival) freedom. Onegin, however, cannot lead her to release, but will destroy any pleasure she may have in domestic stability. This is shown not only by his intrusion into her house in the final scene, but by the use of the house metaphor when Lenskii dies, and his body is described as a 'deserted house' ('opustelyi dom', VI: 32).[46]

Other secondary *topoi* are the duel site, and the graves of Larin and Lenskii, the latter described in some detail with its river placing and two pine trees (VII: 6), a particularly Romantic topography where nightingales sing in the moonlight. Pushkin harps back to his main theme: Romanticism renders even death a pleasant 'topography', although the real countryside is not simply the place where Onegin rides, stealing kisses from peasant lasses, or a place of happy domestic winter scenes (see V: 2) with sleighs and crunch- ing snow. The countryside is also the place in which the events described in Tat'iana's dream are situated (Baevskii, 1990: 100). It is a place of greater extremes, of subconscious yearnings (thus the moonlight, a Romantic image, which saturates Chapter III), passion and of violence, the place of Lenskii's death. The surreal animals which populate Tat'iana's dream show a side to nature which contrasts sharply with the domestic goose slipping on the ice (IV: 42) or the Romantic groves silvered with moonlight. Pastoral scenes often contain hidden threat; in the girls' song in Chapter III, for example, pretty berries (cherries, redcurrants and raspberries) become 'weapons' to be thrown at a fickle lover. Tat'iana, waiting for Onegin to reveal her fate to her in Chapter II, is described as an animal in danger (III: 40).[47]

The *topos* of the journey does appear in this essentially static novel; the text indeed begins with a journey, one might argue, as Onegin rushes to his dying uncle's bedside (I: 42). Tat'iana's journey to Moscow and Onegin's journey to his uncle are both motifs of transit, signifying greater restriction, not escape. Onegin will be tied to the bedside of his relative; Tat'iana goes to the crowded salons of Moscow. Even Onegin's journey (the geography of which will not be discussed because of the incompleteness of that section) ends with his return to Moscow, to the feet of society personified by Tat'iana.

Baevskii also refers to a vertical dimension to the text, an 'eticheskoe prostranstvo' (Baevskii, 1990: 111-3), which has some relevance for the prominent textual theme of conventionality versus feeling, or surface area versus the place of the heart. The text can be seen very much, in the context of a lost or restrained vertical dimension, as a text of surfaces. Pushkin is very good at creating a sense of glitter, of surface movement, which contrasts strongly to the static basis below. This is 'pretend' carnival; there is a lot of rushing about, particularly in Petersburg, the place where the text begins (from which Onegin rushes to his uncle's estate) and where it ends (where Tat'iana holds sway as society belle), but no carnival celebration of change and renewal, of death and birth.

Pushkin's ball scenes are masterpieces of noisy bustle. References to noise are frequent in the novel (see V: 25, and V: 29, for example), and Pushkin appeals not only to the visual sense, but to the auditory, and, in his descriptions of food and flowers, to the gustatory and olfactory senses as well. However, little satisfaction with all these sensual distractions appears to be gained, and unsurprisingly, Evgenii grows bored with the life of the *haut monde* and its conventionality, concealed under the bustle. The dance most frequently mentioned is the mazurka, for example: despite the apparent frenzy of flying feet, the dance is for four or eight couples, signifying social 'pairing' and order. This is no real carnival dance. Society never allows real bacchanalia.

Pushkin's depiction of society has been much commented on, particularly by Soviet commentators seeking ideological correctness in the portrayal of an indolent, vacuous, fickle and unpleasant aristocracy by the national poet.[48] Pushkin is adept at creating a sense of hollowness, of puppets twitching at the end of social strings. *Onegin* is arguably the consummate 'social tale', although dissimilar in its mocking self-awareness to the majority of the glossy trifles published during the 1830s and 40s.[49] As Iezuitova has defined the genre, in such tales society is not merely a background to events, but 'a structure-forming component, determining the major conflict, the dynamics, the principles according to which characters are constituted, and the general emotional key of the entire work'.[50] Within the society tale there is usually a naïve, uninhibited heroine, whose advocacy of the George Sandist 'freedom of sentiment' leads her to social indiscretion; but she, too, is paradoxically one of the conventions of this ambivalent genre which both sets society and emotion at risk, while placing both within the bounds of decorum.

Pushkin describes society as pursuing an ideology of surfaces, according to which characters are evaluated only according to rank, money and appearance; Pushkin's contempt for society becomes immediately apparent in Chapter I, in which the young Onegin is easily able to fool his contemporaries into thinking him intellectual once he has dressed his lack of knowledge with a few allusions and epigrams. What saves Evgenii from complete emptiness is, possibly, his sense of fun, which may hint at the carnival tendency which he so brutally suppresses in his later conventional behaviour; as a child his playfulness is mentioned (he is 'rezov', I: 3) and as a young man-about-town he is called a 'prankster', a 'prokaznik' (I: 15). Unfortunately, his playfulness only appears to manifest itself in his expertise at playing the games of love with which society is so eternally occupied. Surface carnival, or game, takes the place of real carnival exuberance. This is a characteristic demonstrated in the scenes of feasting in the text; these moments for carnival communality (and carnality, i.e. uninhibited sensuality) show how the narrator reins in carnival licence before sensuality can run free and allow his teasing text to turn from foreplay into the fertile ritual of regeneration, i.e. carnival climax.

The first description of feasting occurs in the stanzas devoted to Talon's restaurant, where Onegin and other young bloods drink wine, eat bloody roast-beef, truffles, Strasbourg pie (goose-liver pie), which is rather ominously described as 'undecayed' ('netlennyi', I: 16), i.e. fresh, Limburger cheese, golden pineapples and hot cutlets (I: 16-17) before rushing to the ballet, that 'magical region' ('volshebnyi krai', I: 18), where they can lust after the dancers, traditionally easily beguiled from their short and hard lives into liaisons with the aristocracy. The emphasis in this, the first of the feasting scenes, is on sensual excess, rather than elegance (despite the good vintage and expensiveness of the food). This is suggested by the tactile, even slightly off-putting, details of the 'bloody' ('okravavlennyi', I: 16) roast beef, the goose-liver pie which presumably smells rather strong and thus must be called 'fresh', and the cheese, which is a particularly strong-smelling kind. The red of the blood, the gold of the pineapples and harsh yellow of the Limburger, the greasy image of the cutlet in its hot fat ('goriachii zhir', I: 17) and the detail of the dark, unattractive (albeit extremely tasty) truffles combine to create a visually rich scene with undertones of bestiality, of gorging. Paul Schmidt has written interestingly on this feast as a 'metaphor for conquest' (Schmidt, 1990: 17), not only in the sense of military conquest, but of sexual.[51]

Evgenii then moves on to the ballet, which could provide more sensuality (as the references to ballets about passionate women such as Phaedra, Cleopatra and Moina,[52] I: 17, suggest); but the narrator breaks off, withdraws. The magical world of the theatre becomes dimmed when he considers the great names of the past, now gone from the stage; the theatre is now a place not of rapture but of boredom and social lionising. Sensuality quails beneath the 'disillusioned lorgnette' of the narrator (I: 19); and although, when the dancer Istomina comes on, and her feet – ever a stimulus to sexual musing – begin their movements, there is a possibility of the sensual rhythm returning, Onegin soon becomes bored and leaves the theatre.

However, the 'feasting' scene continues, for he goes to a ball. When Evgenii arrives, the emphasis is on light in the midst of darkness: while the rest of the street sleeps, there is one mansion so illuminated it 'glitters' ('blestit'), and the carriage lamps drawing up in front of it cast rainbows on the snow ('radugi na sneg navodiat', I: 27). Will such glittering promise be fulfilled? The sense of heat and colour is continued once he has 'penetrated' the ballroom, which, in I: 28, is described as being full of noise, movement and tactile imagery; there is 'shum i tesnota'; the officers' spurs clink; women's feet fly; and 'heated glances' ('plamennye vzory') fly in their wake, as Pushkin adds to the sense of heat and intrigue. The emotions are a mixture of passion and jealousy, as is suggested when the narrator mentions that the sound of violins is muffled by the jealous whispers of modish young women ('revom skrypok zaglushen/Revnivyi shepet modnykh zhen', I: 28). This scene of hedonism glitters like champagne held to the light.[53]

Like the first section of the extended evening, the dinner, there is an undercurrent of tension and threat, contained in the 'dismembered' image of women's feet on which the narrator focusses; these feet are followed by burning, i.e. consuming glances, while the metallic ring of spurs adds a further note of menace threatening these dainty female appendages. The famous pedal digression which follows not only evokes sensual imagery of water lapping a woman's legs, which the narrator longs to kiss, but also gives rise to a sense of loss, of post-pedal pathos. These wondrous feet have gone, leaving the narrator behind, and slightly bitter, turning away from sensuality into memory and jest, concluding this first scene of potential carnival with the quip that women's words and glances are as 'deceptive', i.e. quick and elusive ('obmanchivyi, I: 34) as their feet. Carnival is deflated by nostalgia and irony. Unsurprisingly, Onegin goes back to a lonely bed where he lies in Oblomovistic boredom while the city wakes up to its daily shop-keeping activities. This pseudo-carnival cannot offer him true release.

The second 'feasting' scene in the novel is placed on the Larins' estate. This is communality of a different kind, most restrained and uncarnivalesque, for the meals are simple, tea is the only beverage mentioned, guests appear to go home early, and are served 'according to rank' ('po chinam', II: 35). In Chapter III, it becomes clear that such evenings, with discussion of the weather and estate affairs, with jam and home-made wine, are not particularly exuberant; but offer domestic comfort, order, contentment, all of which Onegin, of course, finds boring. His unfulfilled appetite turns to 'khandra', or spleen, a type of mental indigestion (note also Tat'iana's 'hunger' for love referred to in her letter to Onegin).

The mood of the Larins' dinners is much the same as that evoked when Onegin drives home after his exertions at the ball, and merchants and shopkeepers are shown going about their early morning business, as smoke curls from chimneys, and the baker opens his shop (I: 35). Such domesticity hides a cruel truth; society trades its daughters, and eats its way through countless dinners. Domestic life on the Larins' estate, expressed neatly in, for example, a brief line referring to 'dushistyi chai' and 'slivki', which conjure up an image of comfortable domestic ritual (III: 37), appears peaceful and happy. Yet Tat'iana is later 'sold off' and there are unpleasant references during the scene of her name-day party to the voracious guests. Society consumes and devours.

Chapter V contains two opposed scenes of feasting; the feast of monsters glimpsed in Tat'iana's dream (V: 16-18), with its grotesque participants, with Tat'iana a frightened guest, and which culminates in a scene of violence; and Tat'iana's name-day feast, with its grotesquely described participants, with Tat'iana an embarrassed and confused focus of attention, and which will the next day culminate in the scene of Lenskii's death. The name-day feast is actually a continuation, as the narrator tells us, (V: 40) of his first ball scene. He returns to the image of the dance, emphasising the leaps, crashing heels and din that the reader noted from the ball in Chapter I.[54] After this ball *interruptus* one might expect climax, as hedonism has its evening, but Onegin and Tat'iana, are not shown dancing together, for Onegin has selected Ol'ga instead.

The carnival scene of the dream feast presided over by the carnival king, the host, Onegin, is mirrored by the feast presided over by Tat'iana, the name-day or carnival queen; the presence of two parallel scenes indicates that there will be no harmony, joining of king and queen, who are separated by that very divide between dream and social intercourse that the juxtaposition of the two feast scenes suggests. Onegin and Tat'iana do appear on the edge of consummation during the dream feast (as Onegin's pushing open of the door behind which Tat'iana is hiding, and his subsequent claiming of her with a shout of 'she's mine' indicate. The scene is interrupted by the arrival of Ol'ga and Lenskii, the 'mirror' pair of the two lovers who are about to engage in intimacy, and representing Romantic and socially legitimised love; it has already been pointed out that Lenskii is prepared to wait until after the marriage to bed Ol'ga (IV: 50). Carnival and society are held in antithetical stasis, and it is small wonder that Onegin's feelings take the form of violence (warped sexual desire) in the revenge he exacts upon Lenskii, his 'social' alter ego. The name-day party is in many ways as grotesque as the feat of monsters, with the odd collection of neighbours who gather to feast, jaws champing violently, upon meat and blancmange, washed down with champagne (one is reminded of the Rabelaisian stress upon devouring mouths), before buzzing like bees into the card-room.

In chapter VII, one finds a brief scene of Tat'iana attending an Assembly, a gathering described in the familiar terms of heat and noise; this fifth feasting scene has young army officers thundering about with the intent to captivate as many young ladies as possible, creating a sense of vast energy and potential. The carnival queen, Tat'iana, is however not presiding over this carnivalesque scene, but is hidden away by a pillar, placed between two aunts – an imprisoned figure, and about to be pinioned by the steady gaze of a certain general. A new carnival king has appeared, but one who is the antithesis of the iconoclastic and non-hierarchical Onegin, being a man whose position is marked by his uniform. This is another parallel feasting scene to the 'true' scene, or feast of monsters, during which true desires are revealed.

The sixth feasting scene is that of the party at which Onegin sees Tat'iana after his time spent travelling. She is now no longer mistress of the carnival, but queen of society. The subsequent evening party at Prince N's, while attended by the usual society stars for whom the narrator has scant respect, is decorous, presided over by Tat'iana, an 'indifferent princess', an 'inaccessible goddess of the luxuriant, majestic Neva' ('Onegin/..zaniat byl.../ ravnodushnoiu kniaginei,/No nepristupnoiu boginei/Roskoshnoi, tsarstvennoi Nevy', VIII: 27), and the incarnation to Evgenii of forbidden fruit (VIII: 27). Not only a carnival queen, but a goddess. Society has triumphed over carnival.

It is no accident that Tat'iana is described as the goddess of the Neva, for water imagery is significant in the text. Pushkin's imagery can be divided into two broad types, the significant and the trifling. In terms of the latter, Pushkin clutters his text with sensual description in order to create a sense of amusing juxtaposition, and of superficial and fragmented glitter. His references to classical texts, or to food and drink, allow the first of these techniques expression; i.e. drinking champagne and drinking the 'poison of desires' (as Tat'iana does, III: 15) form one such ironic pairing. The blood of the roast beef and the champagne drunk at Talon's possibly form another, equally unlikely, liquid pair. Another is the amusing juxtaposition of a comment on the writer and thinker Rousseau, with references to the trivial detail of Evgenii's combs and dressing paraphernalia (I: 24). Pushkin can also focus, in a caricatured way, on details of a character's appearance, describing him (or her) as rather one-dimensional. The characters who come to Tat'iana's name-day party are metonymically represented by certain details (such as their hats, Triquet's pretentious poem, or their children). Characters in general are reified, their attention to their own appearance permitting the narrator to present them in terms of dress and behaviour, catchphrases and poses, rather than thoughts and feelings; thus the young Evgenii knows only how to dress and dance well (note that dress is often foreign, rendering Evgenii even more 'artificial, i.e. non-Russian – he has his 'bolivar' hat and his pantaloons, I: 15, 26). He is represented in I: 4 in terms of hair and dress, his dancing, his French, and his bow; rather like a wound-up doll. Poor Lenskii turns into that Romantic symbol, a tombstone in a pretty landscape (rather like the kind of image that used to be drawn in Ol'ga's album).

The details in Pushkin's work offers contrasts, fragmentation, and sheer poetry – a wealth of beautiful imagery and ideas expressed in a mixture of tactile and abstract language. Clayton offers a basic list of the contrasting images to be found in the work, several of which have already been discussed, such as the oppositions between country and city, freedom and restriction, passion and cynicism, and age and youth, as expressed in the narrator's nostalgic digressions. Clayton adds the opposition between hot and cold, easily apparent in a text which focusses on winter and summer scenes, and refers to associated ideas such as the contrast between spring and fall, or South and North (Clayton, 1985: 180). There is no single particular context from which Pushkin draws his images, although nature is the most frequently used range. It has been argued that Pushkin describes nature in a rather generalised way (see Nabokov, I., 204-5); however, rather it can be said that nature is inherently plastic, and capable of bearing many imprints of wildness, coldness, domesticity and Romanticism.

Tat'iana is associated with spring, freshness, and dawn; she loves that time before day when the stars, whirling in their dance (Pushkin uses the word 'khorovod', referring to the Russian traditional round dance), fade against the pale horizon, light gleams along the edge of the world, and the wind, morning's messenger, begins to blow (II: 28). When she falls in love with Onegin she is described as a seed brought to life by the fire of spring (III: 7). When withering away with blighted love, she becomes a dawning day wrapped with dark storms-clouds ('Tak odevaet buri ten'/Edva rozhdaiushchiisia den', II: 23). This marvellous image combines the natural with the idea of convention; the verb used is 'to dress', as if sorrow is a mourning garment drawn on to stifle love, and symbolise its death. Tat'iana is also associated with animals, i.e. to a timid deer (II: 25), or a deer, pursued by a hunter (V: 30), to a butterfly caught by a schoolboy, or a hare who sees a hunter approaching (III: 40), all images of nature's vulnerability, and, possibly, of sexual conquest. The moon, also associated with Tat'iana, has connotations of her chastity, which are overturned by the hunting/animal imagery of doe and hare, for Diana, the classical huntress (as Tat'iana is when she sends her letter, perhaps) is now the hunted. Imagery drawn from nature is powerfully linked to the sexual theme in the work, a theme which goes far to link together the ideas of play, lack of climax, power and impotence, and pseudo-carnival in the work. The first image in the entire novel is that of a donkey, which, as well as suggesting a link to Krylov's fable, is also an animal symbolic of a cuckold, or mocked swain, with long ears and stupidity (one thinks immediately of Shakespeare's *Midsummer Night's Dream*). If this seems to be stretching the image, then why is the cuckold theme reintroduced a few stanzas later (I: 12, in the reference to Faublas)?

Onegin is described in Chapter I as a flirt, a fop, able to squeeze out the required tear in moments of sentimentality (I: 10), as a Venus masquerading as a man (I: 25) – a point which encourages Lafferière's view of Onegin as gay (Lafferière, 1989: 247). He is also seen in conjunction with water, the female element. The use of the image water in the novel is, like that of the dawn, used to great effect; in the dream sequence the stream ('potok', V: 11) suggests not only crossing a mental or even social barrier which allows her access to her feelings, but can represent the current of feeling itself, which sweeps Tat′iana on in the sexual chase, pursued by the bear, her clothing becoming increasingly disarrayed. Not only is Onegin born on the banks of the Neva, as the poet tells us (I: 2), but in I: 47-8 he is depicted strolling by, or leaning on, the parapet of this river, and musing on past loves. The narrator interpolates references to the Adriatic and the river Brenta, and to a Venetian girl whom he will love in a gondola. In contrast to Evgenii who stands still and pensive, the narrator thinks of freedom (that 'carnival' word) and of travel. Evgenii is passive, unable to journey with the narrator as his father dies, and not long after that, he is summoned to attend his dying uncle. Up to this point Evgenii's dashing to balls and country places have been journeys of custom and response to summons; he is a traditionally passive, 'feminine' figure, called to dance attendance like a nurse or wife on a dying (i.e. impotent) man. What does he find in the country: 'khandra', accidie, which runs after him like a shadow – or like a faithful wife ('Kak ten′ ili vernaia zhena', I: 54). Onegin is the consort of spleen, which saps his vigour and renders him bored and disillusioned. One may note that 'khandra' 'overwhelms' Onegin ('ovladela', I: 38), as if possessing him, or conquering him sexually.

Onegin is therefore a passive, 'female' figure in the text, an unlikely hero. Tat′iana at first glance seems strangely androgynous; a fey spirit, or an 'animal'; Pushkin uses the word 'lan′', or 'doe', to describe her, suggesting that she is an interesting mixture of 'animal' sensuality and spirit. She is determinedly uninterested in traditional 'feminine pursuits' such as stitchery, playing with dolls, associating with her sister's girlfriends, or showing affection towards her parents. Small wonder that Onegin warms to her; he is not the most masculine of men, and indeed one who refers to himself as a 'invalid' in terms of love ('v liubvi schitaias′ invalidom', II: 19), suggesting physical impairment (and an ironic prefiguring of the man Tat′iana does marry, her 'maimed' general). In his portrait of Onegin during his early years, Pushkin emphasises the androgynous nature of the dandy type, who is sexually predatory and 'effeminately' foppish. As Onegin withdraws from society, and from such stereotypically behaviour, he is seen as far less foppish – he falls prey to spleen instead, which saps his ability to love. His occasional indications of interest in passion, when he is described stealing kisses from peasant girls, for example, appear rather chaste, for the kisses are 'fresh' and 'young'('Poroi belianki chernookoi/Mladoi i svezhii potselyi', IV: 38/9); Onegin is still behaving according to conventional models, exercising a form of *droit de seigneur*.

Onegin's attitude to women, and the narrator's, is based on a condescension which hints at misogyny. The flirtatious ways of a dandy are inherently cruel and cold;[55] how typically hypocritical therefore are the comments on capricious society belles who pout arrogant rubbish, who are cold, egoistic, haughty and teasing (I: 42, III: 22-3). When women are not being described as cold, they are merely objects of lust, the passive recipients of male desire and fantasy, the 'subjects' of male creation (the 'milye predmety' referred to in III: 27). The digression on women's feet shows a sensual disregard for women as anything other than objects of desire (feet, after all, are the part of a woman as far from the seat of intellect as you can get), and yet bring us, paradoxically, back to the first, rather defensive view of women as cold and likely to wound. Feet are for trampling or escape, not merely waiting to be cupped within the narrator's eager hand, or displayed for his delight on the ballet stage. Chapter IV opens with a rather condescending statement, suggesting that women are to a degree masochists, loving those who are unattainable, and who used to have an inclination for Lovelace characters (who have now gone rather out of fashion), i.e. for those who would do them harm. Evgenii's indifference to women is stated very clearly (IV: 10); women are seen either as objects of flirtation, or as actors in a boring domestic drama which is described in IV: 15, complete with cold, silently angry husband and unhappy, neglected wife, disappointed with her immovable husband. As the narrator later adds, he, like Onegin, is prejudiced against marriage (he is one of 'Hymen's foes', IV: 50).

Ol′ga is the fairly passive recipient of Lenskii's adoration, her own feelings appearing rather tepid, though complacent (as is suggested when the narrator talks of beauties' absentmindedness while passionate verses are being read to them). The language in which Lenskii discusses his loved one makes it clear that it is Ol′ga's body which takes first place, and her soul the second (or even third place) when he talks longingly of her shoulders and breasts...and her soul ('Akh, milyi, kak pokhorosheli/U Ol′gi plechi, chto za grud'!/Chto za dusha!, IV: 48). Later, he excuses Ol′ga of any blame, although she has, if not encouraging Onegin's advances, been pleased by them, referring to her as a lily attacked by the worm, Onegin (V: 17); he will be her saviour ('spasitel′', VI: 17), once again casting woman in the role of passive receiver of male attention. However, at the end of the text the 'goddess of the Neva' is triumphant over Onegin, seen at her feet; even the tears that Tat′iana sheds do not weaken her resolve to resist him. The final irony of the text lies in the fact that although showing her power, Tat′iana owns herself to be dutifully bound to her husband, i.e. under his dominion.

Nature symbolism, such as the references to animals, the moon and to water, has the most thematic significance in the novel. Usually, however, rather than create a hierarchy of symbols, Pushkin relies on associations which flutter and glide from idea to surface to idea in what is essentially a tactile and textured text. In the duel scene, for example, abstract ideas and images are used on either side of the stanzas depicting the action of the duel itself. In VI: 28, the narrator muses on friendship and dream; in stanza 31, as Lenskii falls, Romantic imagery takes over, followed in stanza 32 with a more original and sincere image, that of the empty house. The actual duel stanzas however are the most striking; in stanzas 29 and 30 the language is precise, prosaic, and the atmosphere created is one of dreadful suspense. At such a time the hearing grows acute, the senses acutely sensitive; thus the sounds used to describe the cocking of pistols 'Gremit o shompol motolok./V granenyi stvol ukhodiat puli/I shchelknul v pervyi raz kurok' ('The hammer clanks against the ramrod/And into the rifled barrel go the bullets/And the cocked trigger clicked for the first time', VI: 29) are particularly evocative. The words replicate the rasping of the hammer against the ramrod, the hard 'g' sound in 'gremit' and 'granenyi' having an ominous edge. The masculine end-rhyme 'motolok/kurok' is marvellously onomatopoeic, with a dreadful finality about the sound, while the description of the powder poured into the pan of the also creates a heightened tension in the atmosphere ('porokh struikoi serovatoi/Na polku sypletsia. Zubchatyi'). Here the internal punctuation, i.e. the full stop in the middle of the second line heightens suspense as the reader almost feels compelled to draw breath before 'Zubchatyi' ('toothed', or 'cogged'). The description of the powder being poured into the pan of the gun is replicated by the s-alliteration of 'struikoi', 'serovatoi' and 'sypletsia', the latter, meaning 'is poured', being a very onomatopoeic verb. The contrast of the soft, slithering sound of the powder, with the hard 'k' in 'polku' ('pan') heightens the feeling of a cold, dangerous weapon. In stanza 30 the first two lines '"Teper′ skhodites′"./Khladnokrovno' ('"Now march towards each other"./Cold-bloodedly') again shows how sound is textured; the brisk command raps out in a line which is rather short on feet – for time is running out. In line 2, in which rhythm and metre have both been distorted (for the line contains only two feet), the dreadful drawling of the word 'khladnokrovno' does make the blood run cold, the disruption of metrical structure prefiguring the destruction of natural order which is to come with Lenskii's death.

6. Influences and allusions

Despite the apparent Byronic/Romantic influence, it has been argued that the dissimilarities between the work of Pushkin and Byron are more marked than their similarities (a point Pushkin himself noted).[56] One stylistic emulation, rather than allusion, which has been suggested is that of Sterne's digressive masterpiece *Tristram Shandy* (1760-7), with its bizarre, parodic digressions which belie both the realist and the romantic ideas of plot. However, Romanticism is indisputably the textual dominant, intermixed with sentimentalist strains. The most disillusioned Romantic of them all, Byron, is mentioned repeatedly (I: 56, III: 12, and VII: 19); Evgenii is described as dressed like Byron (IV: 37). Onegin keeps a bust of the author in his study, and, as Tat'iana learns from reading through his books (VII: 22), Byron's *Giaour* (1813) and his *Don Juan* (1819-24) have strongly influenced Evgenii's worldview.[57] Evgenii is less like the philandering and ardent Juan, or the passionately vengeful hero of *Giaour*, than Byron's Childe Harold (1812-18), and unsurprisingly, Evgenii is compared to the latter directly three times (and, indirectly, twice), beginning in I, 38, in which a direct comparison is made. He is referred to as a 'Muscovite in Harold's coat' (VII: 24).[58] Even when Evgenii has theoretically 'matured' by his time away from Russia he is still spoken of in terms of Byron (VIII: 8, 'Chem nynche iavitsia? Mel'motom...Garol'dom'?). Evgenii, like Harold, is a dreamer who 'gives himself to pensive idleness' ('vdalsia v zadumchivuiu len'', IV, 44), who can pose as well as an outcast not meant for happiness (IV, 14).

Of all the Romantic pattern-cards on which Evgenii might have modelled himself (he might have been as passionate as Saint-Preux, Malek-Adhel, de Linar, Léonce, or Werther, or as insufferably noble as Sir Charles Grandison), it is interesting that the Byronic mode, with its overtones of brooding self-absorption, is his chosen fashion. Tat'iana, whose reading focusses on the noble, Grandison type of hero mentioned above (see the commentary on the reading stanzas, III, 9-12) is looking for the wrong Romantic hero; Onegin 'verno byl ne Grandison' (III, 10).[59] However, the contrast between Grandison, and Lovelace,[60] the two most famous of Richardson's heroes (the favourite author of Tat'iana's mother and aunt; see Chapter 2, stanza 30), provides two poles (the noble and the base) in terms of which Evgenii is unjudgeable – for he is both, and neither. He is more akin to today's 'heroes,' as the narrator says, pretending to be saddened by the lack of moralism in today's Byronic texts in which (III, 12) one finds negative types such as vampires, Melmoth (mentioned above, VIII: 8, in terms of his materialism), the eternal Jew (an accursed man), Byron's disaffected and rather 'Napoleonic' Corsair, and the slightly demonic leader of a band of brigands, Jean Sbogar; even the seducer Lovelace is out of fashion (IV: 7) amongst this band of sinister types.

The alienation theme suggested by the *Harold* allusions is also brought out in the references to Griboedov's *Gore ot uma* (VI: 11 and VI: 46; VII: epigraph; VIII: 13); the last of which directly likens Onegin to Griboedov's protagonist, the socially alienated Chatskii. Another Romantic 'prototype' for Onegin, alongside those of the Byronic hero and the Griboedovan socially alienated man, is the hero of Benjamin Constant's *Adolphe* (1816) (see Akhmatova, 1974, Hoisington, 1977, Riggan, 1977).[61] Pushkin establishes his main character both as superfluous man and literary parody; essentially a poseur who does not recognise his chance for happiness, preferring to take refuge in the Byronic role of a man dissatisfied with this far-from-ideal world. The superman/Napoleonic idea, suggested in the epigraph to the novel, by the fact that Onegin keeps a bust of the statesman in his study, and in the general references to Napoleon (II: 14, VII: 37), combines with Byronic egoism quite well. The comparison of Evgenii with the philandering Faublas (I: 12) and with a 'Demon' (VIII: 1, 12) is another detail in this unsavoury yet mesmerising picture of a transgressor. Evgenii's later attempts to improve his mind by reading a variety of more sober texts than Byronic works, i.e. historical, philosophical and medical texts (see the commentary to VIII: 35) do not help him to bear his disappointments and become more acceptable to society, now symbolised, ironically, by Tat′iana.

If Onegin is a Harold with overtones of the superman, neither a Grandison nor a Lovelace but a little of both, then Tat′iana is a Clarissa, Harriet Byron, or any of the many other heroines of Romantic literature, with a difference. Her piety is not particularly developed, in contrast to the sentimental excessively virtuous young ladies such as Clarissa and Harriet, or those found in the pages of the works by Rousseau, de Staël, *et al;* neither is she depicted, as Clarrisa and Harriet are, as virgins at the mercy of rampaging men whose passion usually spills over into violence (abduction and rape, in Richardson's novels). Tat′iana is no shrinking lily, but a pagan, with her superstitions and her love of the countryside. In this, she is not a particularly strong example of the heroine of the society tale.[62] Indeed, one surprising feature is that of the lack of references to the Bible in the work, although Clayton suggests a biblical association in terms of the image of the cup in the final stanza (Clayton, 160); Mitchell (1968) also points out the superstitious Tat′iana's lack of Orthodox religion. In the society which Pushkin depicts, a religion of Romantic idolatry has developed; the world is created through fiction, not through an understanding of the grim reality of death – as the treatment of Lenskii's death suggests.

The links with Zhukovskii's sentimental ballad *Svetlana* (III: 5; V: epigraph; V: 10) place her in a folkloristic context (Gukovskii, 1957,

Slominskii, 1959), one more Russian than her reading would initially seem to allow.[63] The reference to the fable by Krylov ('osel byl samykh chistykh pravil') in I, 1, as well as defining the attitude of the young Onegin to his uncle (the 'donkey') very neatly, also gives a Russian flavour to the very first stanza of the work. The references to divination customs, to the simple life of the Larins, who observe old Russian customs (see the commentary to II: 35); the scenes between Tat'iana and her nurse, and the girls' song in Chapter III also add to the base structure of 'Russianness', the contrast between which and Western Romanticism need not be elaborated. It can further be noted however that Clayton has argued for a Shakespearean element, in *Onegin*, contrasting in his chapter on Tat'iana's character the notion of a 'Juliet' theme (noted by other critics in terms of the relationship between Tat'iana and her nurse,) and the 'Princesse de Clèves' theme. Referring to Madame de Lafayette's 1678 novel about a marriage of convenience, Clayton argues that Tat'iana's story describes a transition from Juliet to Princesse, 'from young girl seeking out happiness in love to mature woman rejecting the possibility of that happiness' (Clayton, 130). The Shakespearean theme is echoed in Lenskii's story, when the young student – stuffed with Kantian philosophy (II: 6) i.e. with idealism, and with Romantic dreams, Schiller and Goethe (Schiller is mentioned also in VI: 20), romance the stuff of his reading (II: 9) – is shown staring at Larin's tombstone and quoting from *Hamlet* (II: 37).

There are many other literary references, usually for purposes of gentle mockery of overblown description or sentimentality. Viazemskii has his Romantic verses parodied in VII: 1 (his poem 'Pervyi sneg' is mentioned twice; I: epigraph; V: 3). There are references to the Romantic stanzas of Baratynskii (V: 2-3; VII: epigraph), to the sentimental poet Ivan Dmitriev (1795) (IV: 33; VII: epigraph), to Lomonosov, whose overblown description of the dawn is parodied in the line 'Zaria bagrianoiu rukoi' (V: 25); and there is a mocking reference to Mikhail Murav'ev's 'Bogine Nevy' which has Evgenii leaning on the Neva parapet pensively like a typical dreamer (I: 48). There are also allusions to Pushkin's own rather romantic poetry – *Ruslan i Liudmila* (I: 2), his *Kavkazskii plennik* (I: 57), *Zhenikh* (V: 17), to his *Demon* (VIII: 1, 12 – see Nabokov, III: 129) and to his *Bakhchisaraiskii fontan* (I: 57 and in 'Onegin's Journey'). Apart from such parodic moments, there is also a detectable influence of Pushkin's friend, the poet Gnedich, on the Petersburg descriptions (I: 47), while in his mourning of the state into which the theatre has fallen, Pushkin refers to theatrical figures such as the playwrights Fonvizin, Kniazhnin, Ozerov, and Shakhovskoi, the poet and critic Katenin, the actress Semenova, and the choreographer Didelot (I: 18).

All these allusions continue the idea that *Onegin* is an extended commentary on Romantic literature – and to literature and culture in general; allusions to Dante (Picccchio, 1976) and Chateaubriand (Barratt, 1972) are also notable. In Chapter II, we have a paraphrase of a comment of Chateaubriand's, that 'privychka svyshe nam dana;/Zamena schastiiu ona' (stanza 31),'j'avais la folie de croire encore au bonheur, je le chercherais dans l'habitude' (from Chateaubriand's *René,* 1802). The writer is mentioned again (IV: 26), again in the context of moral encomium, while the epigraph to IV by Jacques Necker, also refers to morality ('morality is in the nature of things'), suggesting that life, human beings, presumably, act according to ethical principles. Such comments are, however, in the minority amidst romantic allusions. The reference to the 14th-century Italian poet Petrarch, famed for his love sonnets to Laura, perhaps extends this romantic line, although the quotation from his *In vita di Laura* (VI: epigraph) is not overtly emotional. In I: 49 love and Petrarch are clearly linked when the narrator talks of travel to Italy and Venice, and of riding in gondolas, learning the language of Petrarch from a young Italian maiden; in I: 58 love and Petrarch again form a pair. More telling in the creation of a Romantic text are the periphrastic, purple passages which imitate the overblown excesses of the sentimental style, and which are acerbically contrasted to the more prosaic interjections made by the narrator (the most telling being the contrasts between the statements made about the duel in VI, where Lenskii's poetic rhetoric is contrasted with the last line of stanza 17). Other cultural references include the mention of the French dramatists, Corneille and Racine, and, in addition to the Romantic prose writers already referred to in the context of Tat'iana's reading, the lesser known M. Grim and August Lafontaine. James Macpherson's pseudo-Celtic legend poems, *Fingal* and *Ossian*, are also referred to briefly (see Nabokov, II, 80, 120 and 254 for comment on the Ossianic theme), and the Italian painter Albani.

Classical references enter the text very early. I: 2 contains a line to Zeus's will (by means of which Evgenii inherits his uncle's estate, as the narrator jocularly remarks).[64] Classical allusions are used in either of two ways; to create ironic contrasts, or a Romantic musing and 'antique' atmosphere, which is used, again, for purposes of parody, or, paradoxically, for creativity. The lyre's voice is more easily heard in the country (I: 56). Evgenii's knowledge of the classics is somewhat limited (II: 6-7 makes it clear that he knows little of Juvenal's satires, Virgil's epic *Aeneid*, the poetry of Theocritus or Homer), and he knows little more about Romulus, i.e. Roman history, but prefers, instead of scholarship, or the wisdom of the ancient Greeks and Roman, to learn a bit about Adam Smith's materialist ideas. Note the amused comment that some ladies like to quote from the bourgeois liberal Say and the jurist Bentham (I: 42), apparently another example of dressing up one's behaviour. The comment that Evgenii is good at 'Ovid's passions' (I: 8) is again ironic, for Evgenii knows only how to play at love.

The gap created between the ideal classical past and the present superficial parody of classical scholarship is highlighted by the description of

Evgenii's trip to the ballet, during which the narrator mourns the departed 'goddesses' (I: 18) whom he remembers from earlier days. The note of mourning sounded for the lack of a Russian Terpsichore reinforces the bathos (I: 20), although Dunia Istomina does drift like down from the lips of the Wind-god Aeolus (I: 20). The theatre audience itself, reacting indiscriminately to theatrical production and ballets, as well as the apparently second-rate nature of such productions, dressed up in cheap showmanship with cupids, snakes and devils (I: 22), provide other examples of how great the gap is between art and imitation, between greatness and parody, ideal and reality.

Onegin himself is described ironically as being as 'podobnyi vetrenoi Venere' (I: 25), though not in terms of goddess-like qualities but 'womanly' vanity, due to the hours spent dressing and preening before his mirror. Tat'iana is compared obliquely to Helen of Troy (although, as Clayton suggests, it is more likely that Ol'ga is the Helen, over whom suitors fight, 134) in the omitted stanza 37.[65] There is also an ironic reference to Homer's descriptions of feasts in the *Odyssey* (which contrast rather strongly with the domestic feast – as described in the often omitted stanzas – held on Tat'iana's nameday, V: 36), allusions which make Onegin's ridiculous duel fought over a woman he does not care for, more petty by contrast to the epic Trojan wars (and feasting) described by Homer. Nina, the society belle, is called the 'Northern Cleopatra' (III: 16), although no men appear to be fighting over her. Zaretskii, likened to the brave Roman general Marcus Atilus Regulus, and to the Roman poet Horatius (VI: 5, 7), is another parodic character in this bathetic yet tragic little war, or duel, of the emotions. Another minor example occurs when Hymen, the Greek god of marriage (IV: 50) is unsurprisingly mentioned in respect of Lenskii's forthcoming nuptials, but the same stanza contains a more prosaic reference to Lafontaine, the novelist of family tales). The references in Chapter VII to the philosopher Epicurus and the Trojan king Priam again are intended to provide a contrast between the classical past and its sages and heroes, and the contemporary 'country Priams' ('derevenskie Priamy', VII: 4) of Pushkin's day, while the Russian 'Automedons' referred to in VII: 35 are clearly not very like their namesake, Achilles' charioteer, in Homer's *Iliad*, nor are Russian ladies, despite their seductiveness, Circes, as the reference to Homer's enchantress might suggest (VII: 27).

Secondly, many of these classical allusions, such as the references to Tasso's Armida (I: 33), his octets (I: 48), Diana's breasts and Flora's cheeks (Pushkin uses the Church Slavonic word 'lanity', instead of 'shcheki', I: 32)[66] are tossed into the stanza in a Romantic, effusive way, creating a sense of overblown poeticism, and are usually contrasted with a more down-to-earth sensuality (as in I: 32, when the narrator forsakes Diana's breasts and Flora's cheeks – for feet). A different kind of manipulation of classical references, although to the same effect, is suggested when the narrator talks of neglecting his Cicero, that greatest of Roman orators, for the less cerebral delights of Apuleius' bawdy texts (VIII: 1). Nature is usually the focus for such classical insertions, and often with the intent of creating a sense of antiquity, passing time, and death. Such descriptions contrast amusingly with Pushkin's more prosaic, even domestic depictions of geese, puppies and people going about everyday countryside tasks. Flowers are referred to frequently, and are either fresh or withering (Lenskii, for example, is referred to in terms of a flower which has withered ('tsvet prekrasnyi/uvial', VI: 31); autumn is used to refer to mortality (VII: 1-3) . The evening star is referred to by its Latin name, Vesper (VI: 24), giving a sense of age as well as approaching darkness; the garden on Evgenii's inherited estate is a 'priiut zadumchivykh Driad' (II: 1), who might be as still as a group of figures on a tomb (in addition to these tree-nymphs, sea-nymphs appear in III: 4). Lenskii's album for Ol′ga has landscapes with a 'nadgrobnyi kamen', khram Kirpidy/Ili na lire golubka (IV: 27), a typical Romantic view with a classical temple dedicated to the Greek goddess of love and beauty (tombstones make an appearance also in stanza 29, again in the context of Romantic albums). References to Lethe, the river of death and forgetting, appear three times, with Lenskii's pre-duel Romantic ponderings (VI: 22) and the allusion in VII: 11 providing an ominous double echo of II: 40 (Morpheus, the Greek god of sleep, is also mentioned, VIII: 28). The reference to Fortuna (I: 45) is another typically Romantic concept, of men's lives being ruled by blind chance which dashes mankind's hopes of happiness. This particular allusion, however, like the epigraph to III, which suggests that Tat′iana is like Echo, hopelessly in love with Narcissus, may when combined offer the more serious idea that man's egoism is the greatest bar to his happiness; here classical references, like the allusions to death, create a philosophical undertone to this lively work.

Nature can be depicted purely in Romantic terms, with classical allusions thrown in to give a more high-flown sound. The moon is often referred to in terms of the mood-goddess Diana (see VI: 2, when Tat′iana sits 'ozarena luchom Diany), or the Neva reflects the 'lik Diany' (I: 47). Lenskii's verses are filled with roses and far-off lands. Unsurprisingly, Onegin refers to Lenskii's Ol′ga as a 'Phyllida' (III: 2), referring to the traditional shepherdess figure which appears in much of Romantic pastoral poetry. Sometimes such allusions are joined to the theme of poetic inspiration; the invocation to the Brenta and the Adriatic, water 'sviat dlia vnukov Apollona' (I: 49) and to the narrator and the 'Albion lyre' in the same stanza (a presumed reference to Byron, the Albion, or English poet) suggest a search for such inspiration (note that Lenskii's poetry is referred to more bathetically as 'groans 'on the *tsevnitsa*, a type of lyre, II: 22). The mention of Phoebus, the Greek god of poetry, called Apollo by the Romans, ('Febrovy', III: 13), and to the Muses

(Aeonids) (II: 9 and II: 40) is a part of this Romantic baggage, while classical nymphs, dryads and naiads also can be glimpsed. Melpomene, Thalia and Terpsichore (VII: 50), the Muses of Tragedy, Comedy, and Dance (see also the comment on Istomina above) make brief appearances (Terpsichore is mentioned in I: 19 and I: 32; see also VI: 39). A specifically poetic muse lines up as well in VII: 1 (she is described as saucy, 'rezvaia', VIII: 3) in VIII: 4 she travels with the poet/narrator, appears to him in far-off places (VIII: 5), and is taken to a society party ('raut') in VII: 6 – it appears that this source of inspiration turns into Tat'iana, or any young society damsel, along the way. The reference to Apuleius in VIII: 1 suggests that she is initially rather a sensuous muse (and is preferred by the narrator to boring old Cicero). The donkey image prominent in Apuleius' most famous work, *Metamorphoses*, also entitled *The Golden Ass*, provides a nice echo of Chapter I and the Krylovian donkey.

Apart from the Romantic note, Pushkin also sounds a more topical one, referring to his contemporaries and friends, such as Viazemskii, Kaverin, or Delvig, drunk at a dinner (VI: 20); or Shishkov, to women he has admired or known, such as the dancer Dunia Istomina (II: 20; V: 37), or Zizi Vul'f (V: 32) There are contemporary references to watch-makers, gunsmiths, restaurateurs, which add a prosaic and realistic underpinning to the Romantic froth. The scenes of balls, evenings at the ballet, and the mention of popular operas (such as the *Dneprovskaia rusalka* 19th-century fantastic opera from which a young lady sings in (II: 12; see also the reference to a Freishütz , III: 31) add to the sense of enjoyment to be derived from the novel, imparting a certain 'carnival' frenzy.

7. Themes

What did Pushkin want to say in *Evgenii Onegin*? A summary of critical approaches, given in no particular order, so far indicates that the follow themes are present: love; social convention; death; the idea of reality, created through the conjunction of differing prose styles (Bocharov has suggested that 'in the relationships between words a structure of the relationship of the word to the world is created, a gnoseological structure of reality', 1974: 66-7); the associated concepts of 'life as novel'[67] and the clash of 'poetry and prose'; romantic disillusionment; another idea is that of poetic craftsmanship, in terms of which the text is really about a writer's development.

Given that the text appears to be about that most basic and all-embracing of ideas, i.e. how characters apprehend reality, then it is tempting to take the idea of comprehension itself as the major theme. The tensions and oppositions in the work suggest that at each and every point in the text there is some attempt being made to frame an idea, a thought, a person (as Tat'iana believes she can understand Onegin by looking between the covers of a book), or to escape from boundaries, or 'frames' (ties of affection, isolation, etc.). Clayton touches upon the idea when he refers to spatial boundaries (Clayton, 1985: 166) and to Onegin's desire to 'step beyond' conventions (Clayton, 1985: 150) as well as time's boundaries (Clayton, 1985: 185), a movement possible only through poetry; Todd (1986) in his discussion of cultural convention or 'determinism', within which the characters strive for autonomy has also contributed to the idea, as has Bocharov, writing of boundaries between viewpoints and prose styles (and the 'translations and switchovers' between the two).

The 'positive' themes that Pushkin offers the reader, ones in which we see the attempt to find harmony and happiness, such as love, the joy of reading, the joy of nature, and friendship, are all thwarted by parallel 'negative' themes. Love leads to indiscretion and to violent denial of love. Pushkin opposes the conventions of the society tale, with its ambivalent attitude towards passion, to Romantic idealism, in terms of which the cult of sensibility is all-important. The joy of reading leads to naïvety and the aping, whether unconsciously or consciously, of behaviour patterns established in literature. Even the pleasure to be found in nature is spoiled by the sentimentalist overlay imposed upon it by those who seek to make nature into a Platonic wellspring which waters idealist sentiment. Friendship is easily destroyed, again by conventionality, which leads Lenskii and Onegin to behave like characters from a society tale or a sentimentally tragic novel. These themes are finely balanced to ensure that the reader comprehends that there will be no resolution of conflict, no discovery of life's unity, of that greater reality which Pushkin's characters strive to know and fail to understand. The reader is left with openness, with a text which defies categorisation or thematic conclusion. The lasting impression to be gained is of the desire to break free from the problem which the balance of themes outlines – namely, that every attempt to find truth leads to falsity, that life itself is permanently overlaid by a conventional simulacrum created either by society or by fiction. Mystery, fragmentation, dichotomy and falsity (all themes suggested by Bocharov's gnoseological approach) combine thematically (and stylistically) to suggest that Pushkin's text lends itself to yet another paradox; a Romantic parody, Onegin is after all concerned with that most romantic of concepts, the reconciliation of opposites (or the 'idealistic dialectic') within a climactic and perfect unity. And this cannot be achieved, as the abrupt ending, with its tragic irresolution of the problems of this passionate pair, clearly indicates.

Yet such a thematic summary suggests a text of sadness, of frustration, and the joy of *Onegin* lies in its scurrilous chatter, its irony, its gentle mockery and whimsically witty depictions. In this way the text attempts to reach beyond convention, to tap that wellspring of joyful vitality which is the essential core of a carnival text. Like *Onegin*, carnival texts are boundary texts, for such novels point to the need to transgress limitations, to move into a glorious cathartic madness, to tear off all masks. Pushkin's text teeters teasingly on the brink of carnival, never quite throwing itself from the balanced simulacrum of static dichotomies. Carnival laughter is heard – this is what makes the text so delightful, so iconoclastic; and yet the laughter fails to broaden into the belly-laugh of the bawdy. However, Pushkin has in his almost-but-not-quite carnival text given us one of the 'essential forms of truth concerning the world': the knowledge that freedom is out there – but always ungraspable. Only in laughter do we gain a sense of that carnival core, for laughter echoes through the conventionality. Is *Onegin's* theme that of the failure of laughter to do more than point the way, while suggesting that the way can never be followed to its end?

Notes to Part Three

1. Pushkin completed the major part of the text on September 25, 1830. In October, 1830, he composed the cancelled Tenth Chapter and revised Chapter VIII in October, 1831, completing Onegin's letter, and moving the section dealing with the Journey to an appendix. See Nabokov, II, 66-7.

2. James Woodward also points to the paradoxes of the text, such as the contradictory comments made of Tat'iana in III: 26 and V:4, as well as the location of her letter, which moves from the narrator's posession to that of Onegin. See Woodward (1982): 25.

3. See A. Razorenov, *K neokonchennomu romanu* '*Evgenii Onegin*', *soch. A. Pushkina, prodolzhenie i okonchanie* (Moscow, 1890). The latest continuation is Evgenii Bashnin's *Fantazii na temu* "*Evgeniia Onegina*" (Colophon, 1992). There are many other works which have been influenced by, or which allude to, *Onegin*. See B. van Sambeek-Weideli, *Wege eines Meisterwerkes; Die russische Rezeption von Pushkin's Evgenij Onegin* (Bern, Peter Lang, 1990; *Slavica Helvetica*, vol. 34), pp. 435-88. See also L. Leighton, 'Marlinskij's *Ispytanie.* A Romantic rejoinder to *Evgenii Onegin', Slavic and East European Journal* 13 (1969), 200-16. One of the more hilarious responses is that by W.W. Rowe; see his 'Onegin Up-to-Date', *Russian Literature Triquarterly* 3 (1972), pp. 452-3; the reader might also find of interest Vikram Seth's *The Golden Gate* (New York/London, Faber & Faber, 1986), a Californian novel written in the Onegin stanzaic form. See also footnote 17, Part I, for Maiakovskii's response to the text. There are rumours of a forthcoming 'sequel': 'Thought to be on their way are novels..carefully tailored to upbeat demands...In *Eugene Onegin* II (aka Sleepless in Sebastopol), "Gene" Onegin did not after all kill Lensky in their duel (that primitive bulletproof vest served its purpose), and on his return from exile discovers that Tat'iana's stuffy husband has fortuitously perished in a multiple *droshky* pile-up' – 'The Loafer', *The Guardian*, 8 March, 1996, p. 15. I am grateful to Michael Pursglove for finding this reference.

4. See Gary Schmidgall's chapter on the opera in his *Literature as Opera* (New York, OUP, 1977), pp. 217-46, Nicholas Zekulin, 'Evgenii Onegin: The Art of Adaptation, Novel to Opera', *Canadian Slavonic Papers*, 29 Nos. 2-3 (1987), 279-91, and Tony Briggs, 'The Blasphemous Masterpiece: Tchaikovsky's Adaptation of *Eugene Onegin*' (Belfast, Queen's University, 1995).

5. Tynianov's belief in the integral nature of the 'Journey' section was later developed by M. Chumakov, in an essay in 1970 ('Sostav khudozhestvennaia teksta Evgeniia Onegina').

6. On September 26, 1830, Pushkin jotted down a scheme for the novel, indicating where the separate sections had been written:

Part I			
Chapter 1	Khandra Kishinev,	Odessa	1823
Chapter 2	Poet	Odessa	1824
Chapter 3	Baryshnia	Odessa Mikhailovskoe	1824
Part II			
Chapter 4	Derevnia	Mikhailovskoe	1825
Chapter 5	Imeniny	Mikhailovskoe	1825, 1826
Chapter 6	Duel'	Mikhailovskoe	1826
Part III			
Chapter 7	Moskva	Mikhalovskoe, Petersburg Malinniki	1827, 1828
Chapter 8	Stranstvie	(Puteshestvie) Moskva, Pavlovskoe, Boldino	1829, 1830
Chapter 9	Svetskii mir	Boldino	

In October, at Boldino, Pushkin also wrote several stanzas of the so-called 10th Chapter.

7. Brown argues that the so-called probem of incompleteness is unimportant; see W.E. Brown, *A History of Russian Literature of the Romantic Period* (Ann Arbor, Ardis, 1988), vol. 3, pp. 65-83 (p. 66); Blagoi has also argued that the novel is finished; see his *Masterstvo Pushkina* (Moscow, Sovetskii pisatel', 1955), pp. 178-198 (p. 181).

8. For more information on Onegin's political leanings, see V.V. Pugaev, 'Onegin-dekabrist ili Onegin "chadaevets"?: K sporam o X glave "Evgeniia Onegina"', *Studia Slavica Academiae Scientarium Hungaricae*, 37, Nos. 1-4 (1991-2), 273-85.

9. A useful work for the reader interested in the concept of textual closure is Frank Kermode's *The Sense of an Ending: Studies in the theory of fiction* (New York, OUP, 1967).

10. *Tvorchestvo Fransua Rable i narodnaia kul'tura srednevekov'ia Renessansa*, written in the 1930s and 40s, published only in 1965. Quotations taken from the book on Rabelais will refer to the useful English translation, which is more readily available to the reader: *Rabelais and his World* (trans. H. Iswolsky) (Bloomington, Indiana University Press, 1984). Bakhtin's ideas on 'carnival' were also developed in his 'Formy vremeni i khronotopa v romane' (1938-9/1975), 'Epos i roman' (1941/1970) and in *Problemy poetiki Dostoevskogo* (1929/1963 – reprinted 1972).

11. Useful works on Bakhtin are: M. Bernstein, 'When the Carnival Turns Bitter: Preliminary Reflections Upon the Abject Hero', in *Bakhtin, Essays and Dialogues on his Work* (ed. G.S. Morson) (Chicago/London, University of Chicago Press, 1986), 99-122; K. Clark. & M. Holquist, *Mikhail Bakhtin* (Cambridge, Mass., Bellknap/Harvard, 1984); and G. Morson & C. Emerson, *Mikhail Bakhtin. Creation of a Prosaics* (Stanford, Stanford University Press, 1990).

12. M. Bakhtin, *Problemy poetiki Dostoveskogo* (Moscow, Khudozhestvennaia literatura, 1972), p. 215.

13. W. Rowe, in his analysis of 'impatient expectation', outlines instances of expectation, but without developing the idea onto the sexual level. See his section on the subject in *Nabokov and Others, Patterns in Russian Literature* (Ardis Ann Arbor, 1979), pp. 20-23. Several other critics have noted an erotic element in Tat'iana's dream; see Nabokov, Müller, and Matlaw.

14. 'It is striking that Tat'iana's dream should have ended with a scream that has been alternatively interpreted as the running through of Lenskii with a knife or Tat'iana's penetration by Onegin', J.D. Clayton, 'A Feminist reading of *Evgenii Onegin*', pp. 262-3. See also Richard Gregg's comment on Tat'iana's fear of sex, and of the knife wielded during the dream as a phallic symbol.

15. See Michael Katz's comments on Tat'iana, her mother and sister Ol'ga in 'Love and Marriage in Pushkin's *Evgenii Onegin*', *Oxford Slavonic Papers* 17 (1984), pp. 77-89.

16. A. Siniavskii (Abram Tertz), *Progulki s Pushkinym* (London, Collins, 1975). For a discussion on the controvesy which surrounded Siniavskii's opinions on Pushkin, see Stephanie Sandler, 'Sex, Death and Nation in the Strolls with Pushkin Controvery', *Slavic Review* 51, No. 2 (Summer, 1992), 294-308.

17. Though I would not go as far as Richard Gregg, who argues that Tat'iana is a figure of 'sublimation', who suppresses her 'black' and 'white' characteristics. See R. Gregg, 'Pushkin's Narratives and the Hex of Darkness', Slavic Review 48, No. 4 (Winter, 1989), 547-57, p. 554.

18. Emerson argues that the ending to the text, with Tat'iana's rejection, 'didn't happen', i.e. all real interaction between hero and heroine ceases midway through Chapter VIII, for Tat'iana has now become the personification of the Muse (see Emerson, 1995: 14-20). Emerson's argument links strongly to Clayton's view that the theme of poetry in the text is paramount.

19. This idea of Onegin as a 'type' is a concept which has survived into the 20th century criticism; see Nishikov on Onegin as the type of the *lishnii chelovek*; Iu. Nishikov, 'Onegin i Tat'iana', *Filologicheskie nauki* 3 (1972), pp. 16-26 (p. 21).

20. An interesting suggestion by Daniel Rancour-Laferrière is that Onegin 'has rejected Tat'iana for homosexual reasons' (Rancour-Laferrière, 1989: 215).

21. On Onegin's contradictory nature, see also A. Tschudakow, 'O strukture personazha geroia "Evgeniia Onegina"', in *Arion. Jahrbuch der Deutschen Pushkin-Gesellschaft* (Bonn, 1989), 263-7.

22. Matsapura in 1987 argued that Pushkin's rough drafts showed a clear authorial attempt to make Onegin's motivations more clear - an argument which I cannot endorse. V.I. Mastapura, 'Rabota A.S. Pushkina na obrazom Onegina', *Voprosy russkoi literatury: Respublikanskii mezhvedomstvennyi nauchnyi sbornik* 52 (1987), 67-75.

23. Nabokov's idea that that Onegin behaves so oddly in provoking the duel because he is in a kind of dream does not really convince. Pisarev lays the blame for the duel squarely on Onegin, arguing that he killed Lenskii either out of irresponsibility or a craven desire for self-preservation D.I. Pisarev, *Sochineniia v chetyrekh tomakh* (Moscow, 1955-6), iii, p. 333.

24. See M.F. Mur'ianov, 'Portret Lenskogo v "Evgenii Onegine"', *Wiener Slavistische Jahrbüch*, 40 (1994), 75-90, for an analysis of Lenskii's studies abroad.

25. The digressive nature of the narrator has been discussed by Jan Meijer; Ettore Lo Gatto has also written on the subject (1955, 58), but the reader would be well advised to read his work in conjunction with Mitchell's critique (1966). See Shaw (1981: 36) for further discussion of the digressions.

26. Carol Ayers distinguishes five types of social discourse, or social strategies for communication: gossip, education (moral maxims), declarations of love, letters and natural conservation. See C.J. Ayers, *Social Discourse in the Russian Society Tale* (Chicago University, unpublished PhD dissertation, 1994), 65-6.

27. Iu. Lotman, 'Khudozhestvennaia struktura "Evgenii Onegina", *Trudy po russkoi i slavianskoi filologii* 9 (Tartu) (1966), 5-22.

28. A.S. Pushkin, *Sobranie sochinenii* v 10 tomakh (Moscow, Gosizdat, 1959-62), t. 9, p. 77.

29. Monika Greenleaf (developing Zhirmunskii's brief comments on Romantic concepts such as 'fragmentariness' in Pushkin), has discussed the idea of counterpointed worldviews (Greenleaf, 1994: 218).

30. As Vickery suggests, writing that Tat'iana's letter is 'not only a declaration of love, but also a call of (*sic*) rescue from a milieu which, she feels instinctively, can never bring her happiness' (p. 122).

31. See Ayers, p. 107; she argues, however, that Onegin is much broader than a standard society tale, p. 10, p. 108.

32. O. Tsvetkov, *Aspects of the Russian Society Tale of the 1830s* (University of Michigan, unpublished PhD dissertation, 1984), p. 47.

33. Tsvetkov argues that this is the major concern of the society tale.

34. See V. Turbin's discussion of the social significance of the work in the context of the epic genre, 'Evgenii Onegin i *M'y*' (sic), *The Pushkin Journal* 1, No. 2 (1993), 197-212.

35. See also W.W. Rowe's discussion of the 'vivifying force' of 'impatient expectation' created within the work (here he discusses characters' expectation, rather than readers'). See his first chapter in W.W. Rowe, *Nabokov and Others: Patterns in Russian Literature* (Ann Arbor, Ardis, 1979), pp. 15-26.

36. Which Bakhtin called 'zlobodnevnaia publitsistichnost'', *Problemy poetiki Dostoevskogo*, p. 200.

37. See M. Korneeva-Petrulan, 'Zametki o sintaksise Pushkina', in *Stil' i iazyk Pushkina* (ed. K.A. Alaverdov) (Moscow, Uchpedgiz, 1937), 107-12. The book contains a discussion of the concept of 'polnoglasie' in Pushkin's work as well as general articles on his language.

38. See Barry Scherr's discussion of the Onegin stanza in his *Russian Poetry. Meter, Rhythm and Rhyme* (Berkeley/Los Angeles, University of California Press, 1986), pp. 235-7. See also Nabokov, pp. 9-15, and Briggs, pp. 8-27. A more complex analysis can be found in D.S. Worth's 'Grammatical Rhyme Types in *Evgenij Onegin*', in *Alexander Puskin Symposium II* (eds. A. Kodjak, K. Pomorska, K. Taranovsky) (Columbus, Slavica, 1980), pp. 39-48; see also his 'Rhyme Enrichment in Evgenii Onegin', in *Miscellanea Slavica: To Honour the Memory of Jan M. Meijer* (Amsterdam, Rodopi, 1983), pp. 535-42. See also L. Grossman, *Oneginskaia strofa* (Letchworth, Prideaux, 1977) (reprint from 1924).

39. The alternation of masculine and feminine rhymes refers to whether the last syllable in the line is a stressed rhyme (masculine, and designated by a small letter, i.e. 'b'), or whether the rhyme extends over two syllables, the last of which is unstressed (designated by a capital letter, i.e. 'A').

40. See Briggs' Introduction to the 1993 BCP edition of *Evgenii Onegin* for comment on the rhyme scheme, pp. viii-x. Briggs analyses a stanza from the novel (III, 38), pp. x-xiv; see also his *Eugene Onegin* monograph (1992), 8-27, in which he discusses the stanza form and analyses two of them (I, 10, and I, 35).

41. Nabokov uses the 'reverse' *Onegin* stanza in his 'Universitestkaia poema', *Sovremennye zapiski*, 33 (1927), 223-54, the structure of which replicates the *Onegin* stanza but backwards, i.e. it begins with a couplet (gg) followed by a mixed quatrain (EffE), followed by two couplets (CC, DD) and concludes with a mixed rhyme quatrain (AbAb). I am most grateful to Michael Basker for this reference.

42. The fable runs like this: A peasant hired a donkey to drive off the crows and sparrows from his kitchen garden. The donkey is of the most honest principles, unacquainted with cunning and theft, and carries out its duties so zealously that everying within the kitchen garden is trampled flat, thus destroying any possible profit for the peasant, who belabours the beast with a cudgel. The donkey, adds the narrator, didn't act rightly in his lack of generosity towards the birds; but the one who gave him the task of guarding the garden was perhaps more of a fool... Who is the 'fool' in this case? Both society and the uncle – and Onegin as well.

43. Charles Maturin, *Melmoth the Wanderer* (Penguin, 1977), p. 41. See Nabokov, I, 34-5 for comment on the Maturin link, and the link with Byron mentioned next.

44. Other spatial referents do of course occur in the text, usually in connexion with the narrator's, or Onegin's, desire for escape and travel to more Romantic topographies.

45. See V. Turbin's oblique comments on the *topoi* of wood, sky and sea in the novel, and his belief that they show 'prison' characteristics, i.e. demonstrate confinement; Turbin, 1978: 178.

46. 'Opustelyi dom' is a phrase used by Anna Akhmatova in her famous *poema, Rekviem*, about the Stalinist purges.

47. See O.N. Skachkova, 'Peisazh v lirike A.S. Pushkina i v romane Evgenii Onegin", *Wisenschaftliche Zeitschrift der Wilhelm-Pieck-Universität*, 32, No 6 (983), 17-20.

48. The culminating two stanzas of Chapter VI originally contained a very pointed description of a society filled with fools and childike, petty individuals, hypocrites, madmen and the treacherous; these stanzas were later shortened to form one verse, with the strong comments removed.

49. Pushkin's society tales include not only *Onegin*, but 'Pikovaia dama' (1833), a parody of the genre, 'Egipetskie nochi' (1835), the poem 'Graf Nulin' (1825) as well as the fragments 'Russkii Pelam' (1834/5), 'Gosti s"ezzhalis' na dachi' (1829), 'Na uglu malen'koi ploshchadi' (1829) and 'Roman v pis'makh' (1829), as well as 'Vystrel' from the *Povesti Belkina* (1830-31).

50. R.V. Iezuitova, 'Svetskaia povest'', in *Russkaia povest' 19-ogo veka: istoriia i problematika zhanra* p. 173.

51. Schmidt's highly enjoyable article contains the following comment on the first feasting scene: 'All the sense are put to work in this description: the ear...eye...nose...the tactile sense in...the icy chill of a glass, the tearing of hot, succulent flesh from a rib bone, the sweet wetness of a piece of pineapple...this is a poetry of the flesh – one that borders, perhaps, on pornography', p. 19. His comments on the androgynous nature of the pineapple, p. 30, are equally evocative.

52. This female character, from a play based on Macpherson's poem, is perhaps linked to another Macpherson poem, *Malvia*; see Nabokov, II, 120.

53. Champagne appears in IV: 45-6, in which the narrator mourns that his stomach no longer can take Moët, Cliquot, or Ai, but prefers a sedate Bordeaux; see also V: 32-3.

54. The most energetic stanza, 43, is omitted in the BCP edition of *Onegin*; it appears in several of the translations. See Nabokov, II: 545.

55. See D. Millet-Gerard, 'Dandys et "grandes coquettes", de Pouchkine et Balzac a Lermontov', *L'Anne Balzacienne*, 14 (1993), 41-63, on 'female dandyisme' and Tat'iana's lack of this attribute.

56. For further information on possible influences, the reader might consider L. O'Bell's article 'In Pushkin's Library', *Canadian-American Slavonic Studies* 26, No. 2 (Summer, 1982), 207-26.

57. Brown discusses the diferences between *Don Juan and Evgenii Onegin*, p. 67. See also A.V. Belikova, '"Evgenii Onegin" A.S. Pushkina i "Don-Zhuan" Dzh. G. Baïrona – "Romany v stikhakh"', *Vestnik mosk. universiteta. Seriia 9. Filologiia* 2 (1982), 71-8.

58. See Hoisington, 1975, and Vickery, 1963 & 1968.

59. For comment on the influence of *Werther* on *Onegin*, see Peer, 1969, Riggan, 1973. See Stanley Mitchell's comments on the idea found in de Staël and Rousseau, of virtue as a natural religion of the heart in his 'Tat′iana's reading', *Forum for Modern Language Studies* iv, No. 1 (January, 1968), pp. 1-21 (p. 2). He has other comments on Richardson, 8-11, arguing that Tat′iana's heroines, Clarissa, Julie, Delphine – 'seek fortification through religion', whereas Tat′iana is not religious (p. 11).

60. Cizevsky is inaccurate in stating that Grandison is the hero of *Clarissa Harlowe*, p. 23.- it is Lovelace.

61. Evgenii is also likened to another socially frowned-upon type, the philosopher Chaadaev (I: 25). Unlike Chaadaev, however, Evgenii has little philosophy, and so, ironically, he is merely likened to Chaadaev in the way he dresses (I:25). In I: 15 he wears a 'bolivar', a type of hat deriving from the well-known revolutionary's headgear. Pushkin reiterates that Evgenii only *looks* like a free-thinking Bolivar or a Chaadaev.

62. For information on the conventions of the 'novel of worldliness' such as *Clarissa* or *Julie*, see P. Brooks, *The Novel of Worldliness* (Princeton, Princeton University Press, 1969).

63. There is another link to a Russian literary text; her dream has similarities to the dream of Sonia from Griboedov's *Gore ot uma* (see Brodskii, 1957, Matlaw, 1959).

64. In 'Onegin's Journey' there are references to heroic tales from history and myth which will be omitted from this discussion, given the unfinished/censored version of this section.

65. The BCP edition omits this reference; see Charles Johnston's translation, p. 150.

66. In the following stanza, I: 33, Pushkin again uses the word 'lanity', and in the next line, the Church Slavonic 'persi', breasts, instead of 'grudi'.

67. In *Onegin*, Pushkin found a unique artistic territory for himself – 'at the boundary between two realities: Life and the Novel, reality and literature' (Tarkhova, 1978: 16).

Bibliography

1. Primary Literature

Russian versions of Evgenii Onegin

Evgenii Onegin (ed. A. Briggs) (London, Bristol Classical Press, 1993)

Evgenii Onegin (Moscow, Kniga, 1988) (reprint of 1837 edition)

English versions of Evgenii Onegin

Eugene Onegin, trans. by T. Spalding (London, Macmillan, 1881)

Eugene Onegin, trans. by B. Deutsch (New York, 1936; Harmondsworth, Penguin, 1964)

Eugene Onegin, trans. by D. Prall Radin and G.Z. Patrick (Berkeley, University of California Press, 1937)

Evgeny Onegin, trans. by O. Elton (London, Pushkin Press, 1937)

Eugene Onegin, trans. by B. Simmons (London, B. Simmons, 1950)

Eugene Onegin, trans. by W. Arndt (New York, Dutton, 1963)

Eugene Onegin, trans. by E. Kayden (Ohio, Yellow Strings, 1964)

Eugene Onegin, trans. with commentary by V. Nabokov, in 4 vols., (Princeton University Press, 1975), first published in 1964; abridged (2-volume) edition, Princeton, Prineton University Press, 1990

Eugene Onegin, trans. by C. Johnston (Ilkley, 1977; Harmondsworth, Penguin, 1979)

Pushkin's Eugene Onegin (dual-language), trans. by S.D.P. Clough (Oxford, SDP Clough, 1988)

Yevgeny Onegin, trans. by A.DP. Briggs (revision of Elton's 1937 translation) (Everyman, 1995)

Eugene Onegin, trans. with Introduction, by James Falen, (Oxford, OUP, 1995)

2. Secondary Literature

Commentaries

Cizevsky, D., *Evgenij Onegin* (Cambridge, Harvard University Press, 1953)

Brodskii, N.L., *Komentarii k romanu A. S. Pushkina "Evgenii Onegin"* (Moscow, Mir, 1932)

Lotman, Iu. M., *Roman A.S. Pushkina "Evgenii Onegin"* (Leningrad, "Prosveshchenie", 1980)

Nabokov, V., *Evgenii Onegin* (see above)

Critical overviews, bibliographies

Hoisington, S.S., *Russian Views of Pushkin's 'Eugene Onegin'* (trans., ed. S. S. Hoisington, trans. also by W. Arndt) (Indiana, Indiana University Press, 1988)

Meilakh, B. S., 'Spory o Evgenii Onegine v proshlom i nastoiashchem' in his *Talisman. Kniga o Pushkine* (Moscow, Sovremennik, 1975), 239-302.

Usok, I., 'Roman A.S. Pushkina Evgenii Onegin i ego vospriiatie v Rossii XIX-XX v.', in *Russkaia literatura v istoriko-funktsial'nom osveshchenii* (Moscow, Nauka, 1979)

van Sambeek-Weideli, B., *Die russische Rezeption von Pushkins Evgenii Onegin* (Slavica Helvetica 34/5, Peter Lang, Bern, 1989)

——— *'Evgenii Onegin' A.S. Pushkina: Bibliografiia* (Slavica Helvetica 35, Peter Lang, Bern, 1990)

Nineteenth-century Russian Literature in English (comp. C. Proffer & R. Meyer) (Ann Arbor, Ardis, 1990)

Wreath, P. J. & A.J., 'Alekander Pushkin. A Bibliography of Criticism in English', *Canadian-American Slavic Studies*, 10, No. 2 (1976), 279-304

Zelinskii, V. (ed), *Russkaia kriticheskaia literatura o proizvedeniiakh A.S. Pushkina* (v 7-i ch.) (M., Tip. E. Lissnera & Iu. Romana, 1887-1903)

General

(i) Bakhtin

Bakhtin, M., *Tvorchestvo Fransua Rable i narodnaia kul'tura srednevekov'ia Renessansa* (Moscow, 1965) (revised version of 'F. Rable v istorii realizma', 1940)

——— *Rabelais and His World* (trans. H. Iswolsky) (Bloomington, Indiana University Press, 1984)

——— *Voprosy literatury i estetiki* (Moscow, Khudozhestvennaia literatura, 1975)

——— 'Epos i roman', *Voprosy literatury* 1 (1970), 95-122

——— *Problemy poetiki Dostoevskogo* (Moscow, Khudozhestvennaia literatura, 1972)

Bernstein, M., 'When the Carnival Turns Bitter: Preliminary Reflections Upon the Abject Hero', in *Bakhtin, Essays and Dialogues on his Work* (ed. G.S. Morson) (Chicago/London, University of Chicago Press, 1986), 99-122

Clark, K. & Holquist, M., *Mikhail Bakhtin* (Cambridge, Mass., Bellknap/ Harvard, 1994)

Morson, G., & Emerson, C., *Mikhail Bakhtin. Creation of a Prosaics* (Stanford, Stanford University Press, 1990)

(ii) On the 'society tale'

Ayers, C.J., *Social Discourse in the Russian Society Tale* (Chicago University, unpublished PhD dissertation, 1994)

Brooks, P., *The Novel of Wordliness* (Princeton, Princeton University Press, 1969)

Belkina, M.A., 'Sovetskaia povest 30-kh godov i Kniaginia Ligovskaia Lermontova', in *Zhizn' i tvorchestvo M. Iu. Lermontova* (Moscow, Khudozhestvennaia literatura, 1941)

Iezuitova, R.V., 'Svetskaia povest'' in *Russkaia povest' 19-ogo veka: Istoriia i problematika zhanra* (ed. B.S. Meilakh) (Leningrad, Nauka, 1973)

Shephard, E.C., 'The Society Tale and the Innovative Argument in Russian Prose Fiction of the 1830s', *Russian Literature* X-II (1981)

Tsvetkov, O., *Aspects of the Russian Society Tale of the 1830s* (University of Michigan, unpublished PhD dissertation, 1984)

Urbanic, A., *In the Manners of the Times: The Russian Society Tale and British Fashionable Literature, 1820-40* (Brown University, unpublished PhD dissertation, 1983)

(iii) Works influenced by/continuations of Onegin

Deltcheva, R., 'Recycling the Genre: The Russian and American Novel in Verse: The Case of Pushkin's *Evgenii Onegin* and Seth's *The Golden Gate*', *Rosyzska Ruletka* 2 (1995), 33-51

Leighton, L., 'Marlinskii's *Ispytanie*. A Romantic rejoinder to *Evgenii Onegin*', *Slavic and East European Journal* 13 (1969), 200-1

Nabokov, V., 'Universitetskaia poema', *Sovremennye zapiski* 33 (1927), 223-54

Razorenov, A., *K neokonchennomu romanu "Evgenii Onegin" soch. A. Pushkina, prodolzhenie i okonchanie* (Moscow, 1890)

Rowe, W.W., 'Onegin Up-To-Date', *Russian Literature Triquarterly* 3 (1972), 452-53

Seth, V., *The Golden Gate* (New York/London, Faber and Faber, 1986)

'The Loafer', *The Guardian*, 8 March, 1996, p. 15

The most recent major work, A. Briggs' *Eugene Onegin* (1992) includes only a short list of selected articles and books, as does the *Onegin* bibliography in *Nineteenth-century Russian Literature in English* (comp. C. Proffer & R. Meyer) (Ann Arbor, Ardis, 1990). The following Bibliography has therefore aimed at comprehensiveness rather than selective usefulness.

3. Secondary literature (in Russian)

19th-century criticism

Annenkov, P.V., *Materialy dlia biografiia Aleksandra Sergeevicha Pushkina* (Moscow, Kniga, 1985) (reprint of 1855 St. Petersburg edition)

Belinskii, V.G., *Polnoe sobranie sochinenii* (Moscow, Izd. Ak. Nauk, 1953-9); translation of Belinskii's 9th article under the title 'Tat'iana: A Russian heroine', by S. Hoisington, *Canadian-American Slavic Studies* 29, Nos. 3-4 (1995), 371-95

Dobroliubov, N.A., *Sobranie sochinenii v deviati tomakh* (Moscow, GiKhL, 1962)

Dostoevskii, F.M., 'Pushkin. Ocherk. Proizneseno 8 iiunia v zasedanii Obshchestva liubitelei rossiskoi slovesnosti', in his *Dnevnik pisatelia na 1977 god* (Paris, YMCA Press, undated), 510-27

Druzhinin, A.V., 'A.S. Pushkin i poslednee izdanie ego sochinenii', in his *Sobranie sochinenii*, vii (St. Petersburg, 1965), 30-82

Kachanovskii, V., *Aleksandr Sergeevich Pushkin kak vospitatel' russkago obshchestva* (Kazan, Tip. Imperatorskago Universiteta, 1888)

Katkov, M.N., 'Pushkin', *Russkii vestnik* 1-189 (1856)

Kireevskii, I., *Polnoe sobranie sochinenii* (Moscow, 1911), ii, 1-12

Kliuchevskii, V.O., 'Onegin i ego predki', in his *Sochinenii v vos'mi tomakh* (Moscow, Gos. izd. polit. lit., 1956-9), vii; translation, M. Shatz, 'Yevgeni Onegin and His Ancestors', *Canadian-American Slavic Studies* 16, No. 2 (1982), 227-46

Merezhkovskii, D.S., *Vechnye sputniki: Pushkin* (St. Petersburg, 1897)

Miller, V.F., *Pushkin kak poet-ethnograf* (Moscow, 1899)

Miliukov, A.P., 'Evgenii Onegin' in his *Ocherk russkoi istorii poezii* (St. Petersburg, 1847), 167-88

Nekrasov, I.S., *O znachenii Pushkina v istorii russkoi literatury* (Odessa, Tip. Odesskago Vestnika, 1887)

Pisarev, D.I., 'Pushkin i Belinskii', in his *Sochineniia v chetyrekh tomakh* (Moscow, GiKhl, 1956), 306-64

Russkie poety o Pushkine (Moscow, Tip. G. Lissnera & A. Geshelia, 1899)

Strakhov, N.N., *Zametki o Pushkine i drugikh poetakh* (Kiev, 1897/reprinted Hague, 1967)

Turgenev, I.S., 'Rech' po povodu otkrytiia pamiatnika A.S. Pushkina v Moskve', in his *Sochineniia v piatnadtsiati tomakh*, xv (Moscow-Leningrad, Nauka, 1968), 66-76

Venevitinov, D.V., *Polnoe sobranie sochinenii* (Moscow-Leningrad, Academia, 1934)

Voskresenskii, E., *"Evgenii Onegin" A.S. Pushkina (razbor romana)* (Iaroslavl', Tip. Gubernskoi Zemskoi Upravy, 1887)

20th-century criticism

Akhmatova, A., *O Pushkine: stat'i i zametki* (Leningrad, Sovetskii pisatel', 1977)

Baevskii, V.S., 'Struktura khudozhestvennogo vremeni v "Evgenii Onegine"', *Izd. AN SSSR 41*, no. 3 (1982), 204-18

———'Vremia v "Evgenii Onegine"', in *Pushkin. Issledovaniia i materialy*, 11 (1983), 119-28

———'Khudozhestvennoe prostranstvo v Evgenii Onegine', *Izvestiia Akademii Nauk, seriia literatury i iazyka* 44, No. 3 (1985), 213-224

———'Tematicheskaia kompozitsiia "Evgeniia Onegina" (Priroda i funktsii tematicheskikh povtorov)', in *Pushkin: issledovaniia i materialy*, 13 (1989), 33-44

———*Skvoz' magicheskii kristal. Poetika "Evgeniia Onegina", romana v stikhakh A. Pushkina* (Moscow, Prometei, 1990)

Barlas, L.G., 'O kategorii vyrazitel'nosti, i izobrazitel'nykh sredstvakh iazyka', *Russkii iazyk v shkole* 1 (1989), 75-80

Belikova, A.V., '"Evgenii Onegin" A.S. Pushkina i "Don-Zhuan" Dzh. G. Bairona - "Romany v stikhakh"', *Vestnik mosk. universiteta. Seriia 9. Filologiia* 2 (1982), 71-8

Berezhkova, M.S., 'Ekspressiia oneginskoi strofy', *Russkii iazyk v shkole*, 5 (1982), 48-52

Blagoi, D., *Sotsiologiia tvorchestva Pushkina. Etiudy* (Moscow, Federatsiia, 1929)

______'Kritika o Pushkine', in *Putevoditel'* po Pushkinu (Moscow-Leningrad, Goslitizdat, 1931), 189-210

______*Masterstvo Pushkina* (Moscow, Sovetskii pisatel', 1955)

______*Tvorcheskii put'* Pushkina (Moscow, Sovetskii pisatel' 1967), 254-58

Bocharov, S.G., 'Forma plana' (Nekotorye voprosy poetiki Pushkina)', *Voprosy literatury* 12 (1967), 115-36

______*Poetika Pushkina. Ocherki* (Moscow, Nauka, 1974), 26-104

______'Poeticheskie predanie i poetika Pushkina', in *Pushkin i literatura narodov sovetskogo soiuza* (Erevan, Erevanskii universitet, 1975), 53-73

______'Frantsuzskii epigraf k Evgeniiu Oneginu', *Cahiers du monde russe et soviétique* 32, No. 2 (1991), 173-88

Boitar, E., Nikulina, N. (tr.), 'Mekhanizm literatury: Pushkin i Esterkhazi', *Studia Slavica Academiae Scientarium Hungaricae* 28, Nos. 1-4 (1982), 357-70

Bondi, S., *O Pushkine* (Moscow, Khudozhestvennaia literatura, 1978)

Botsianovskii, V.F., 'Nezamechennoe u Pushkina', *Vestnik literatury* 6-7 (1921)

Burtsev, V.L., *Kak Pushkin khotel izdat'* 'Evgeniia Onegina' *i kak izdal* (Paris, Zeliuk, 1934)

Buznik, V., 'Mera klassiki - gumanizm', *Russkaia literatura* 3 (1987), p. 4

Chazarov, G.A., 'Son Tat'iany', *Ars* 1 (Tiflis) (1991), 9-20

Chernov, A., 'Sledovatel' za mysliami velikogo cheloveka', *Znamia* 1 (1987), 135-50

Chudakov, A.P., 'Stat'ia Iu. N. Tynianova "O kompozitsii 'Evgeniia Onegina'", in *Pamiatnik kul'tury, novye otkrytiia: Pis'mennost', iskusstvo, arkheologiia. Ezhegodnik 1974* (Moscow, Nauka, 1975), 121-3

Chumakov, Iu.N., 'O sostave i granitsakh teksta "Evgeniia Onegina"', *Russkii iazyk v kirgizskoi shkole* 1 (1969), 32-3

———'Sostav khudozhestvennogo teksta "Evgeniia Onegina"', in *Pushkin i ego sovremenniki* (ed. E.A. Maimin) (Pskov, LGPI, 1970), 20-33

———' "Otryvki iz puteshestviia Onegina" kak khudozhestvennoe edinstvo', *Voprosy poetiki literaturnykh zhanrov: sbornik nauchnykh statei* 1 (Leningrad LGPI, 1976), 3-12

———' "Den' Onegina" i "Den' avtora"', *Voprosy poetiki literaturnykh zhanrov: sbornik nauchnykh statei* 2 (Leningrad, LGPI, 1976), 3-120

———*"Evgenii Onegin" i russkii stikhotvornyi roman* (Novosibirsk, 1983)

Clayton, J.D., 'Evgenii Onegin: v poiskakh fabuly', *Russian Literature* 23-3 (October, 1988), 303-18

D'iakonov, I., 'O vos'moi, deviatoi i desiatoi glavakh "Evgeniia Onegina"', *Russkaia literatura* 3 (1963), 37-61

Eikhenbaum, B.M., *Skvoz' literaturu: sbornik statei* (S-Gravenhage, Mouton, 1924/reprinted 1962), 157-70

———*O poezii* (Leningrad, Sovetskii pisatel', 1969)

Eikhenval'd, Iu., *Pushkin* (Moscow, IN Kushnerev, 1916), 156-198

Fateeva, N.A., 'Pasternak i Pushkin: Put' k proze', *Russkii iazyk za rubezhom* 4 (1994), 94-104

Fenina, G.V., 'O nekotorykh aspektakh kommentirovaniia Nabokovym romana A.S. Pushkina "Evgenii Onegin"', *Filologicheskie nauki* 2 (1989), 9-18

Fomichev, S.A., 'Iz komentariia k "Evgeniiu Oneginu"', *Vremennik Pushkinskoi komissii* (Leningrad, 1981)

———'U istokov oneginskogo zamysla', *Russkaia rech'* 1 (1992), 10-14

Freilikh, S., 'Parodiia kak priem: O Pushkine i Eizenshteine', *Voprosy literatury* (Rockville), 5 (1991), 117-43

Gershenzon, M.O., *Stat'i o Pushkine (*Moscow, 1926)

Ginzburg, L. Ia. 'K postanovke problemy realizma v pushkinskoi literature', *Vremennik pushkinskoi komissii* (M-L., ANSSR, 1936)

Gofman, M.L., 'Propushchennye strofy "Evgeniia Onegina" in *A.S. Pushkin, Sochineniia* vi (ed. S. A. Vengerov) (Petersburg, 1915)

Gordin, M., 'Velichie "nichtozhnogo geroia"', *Voprosy literatury* (Rockville) 1 (1984), 149-67

Gor'kii, M., 'Istoriia russkoi literatury' (Otryvki), in *A.S. Pushkin v russkoi kritike* (Moscow, Gosizd., 1953), 542-65

Gorovskii, G., 'Dukhovnaia opora', *Literaturnaia gazeta* 21 January, 1987, p. 5

Grechina, O.N., 'O folklorizme "Evgeniia Onegina"', *Russkii fol'klor* 18 (1978), 18-41

Grekhnev, V.A., 'Dialog s chitatelem v romane Pushkina *Evgenii Onegin*', in *Pushkin. Issledovanie i materialy* ix (Leningrad, Nauka, 1979)

Grigor'ev, A.A., *Literaturnaia kritika* (Moscow, Khudozhestvennaia literatura, 1967), 157-203

Grombach, S.M., 'Ob epigrafe k "Evgeniiu Oneginu"', *Izvestiia Akademii Nauk SSSR: Seriia literatury i iazyka*, XXVIII: 3 (1969), 211-19

Grossman, L., *Oneginskaia strofa* (Letchworth, Prideaux, 1924, reprinted 1977)

Gukovskii, G.A., *Pushkin i problemy realisticheskogo stilia* (Moscow, Goslitizdat, 1957)

Gurevich, A.M., '"Evgenii Onegin": Avtorskaia pozitsiia i khudozhestvennyi metod', *Izvestiia akademii nauk SSSR - Seriia literatury i iazyka* 46, No. 1 (1987), 7-19

Hellberg, E. F., 'Kak v zerkale: gadanie i son Tat'iany', *Studia Slavica Finlandensia*, 6 (1989), 1-19

Imre, L., 'Stol' tipichno vengerskii i stol' tipichno russkii: Zhanrovoe vliianie "Evgeniia Onegina" v vengerskoi stikhotvornoi epike', *Studia Slavica Academiae Scientarium Hungaricae* 33, Nos. 1-4 (1987), 149-62

Iskrin, M.G., 'Gadatel', tolkovatel' snov', *Russkaia rech'* 3 (1989), 140-4

———'Otryvki severnykh poem', *Russkaia rech'* 3 (1990), 8-10

Ivanov-Razumnik, R.V., 'Evgenii Onegin', in A.S. Pushkin, *Sochineniia*, iii (St. Petersburg, 1907), 205-34

Khaev, E. S., *Idillicheskie motivy v "Evgenii Onegine"* (Gor'kii, 1981)

Khardzhiev, N.I., 'Kratkaia istoriia "vina komety"', *Russkaia rech'* 4 (1991), p. 8

Khodasevich, V. F., *O Pushkine* (Berlin, Petropolis, 1937)

Korneeva-Petrulan, M., 'Zametki o sintaksise Pushkina', in *Stil' i iazyk Pushkina* (ed. K.A. Alaverdov) (Moscow, Uchpedgiz, 1937), 107-12

Kotliarevskii, N.A., *Literaturnye napravleniia aleksandrovskoi epokhi* (St. Petersburg, 1907), 210-36

Kozhevnikov, V., 'Shifrovannye strofy "Evgeniia Onegina"', *Novyi mir* 6 (1988), 259-66

———'Imela li mesto "rasseiannost'"?', *Novyi mir* 6 (1989), 268-9

———*Vsia zhizn', vsia dusha, vsia liubov'* (Moscow, Prosveshchenie, 1993)

Krasukhin, G., 'Tat'iany milyi ideal: K 150-letiiu vykhoda v svet *Evgeniia Onegina* A.S. Pushkina', *Nash sovremennik* 3 (1983), 175-85

Kurbatov, V., 'Onegin novymi glazami: Graficheskaia Pushkiniana E. Nasibulina', *Literaturnoe obozrenie* 6 (1984), 94-5

Lakshin, V., 'Dvizhenie "svobodnogo romana": Zametki o romane *Evgenii Onegin*', *Literaturnoe obozrenie* 6 (1979), 17-24

Latsis, A.,'"Dikie utki", i ne tol'ko!', *Voprosy literatury* 12 (1988), 254-59

Lazurkova, M., 'Vremia v romane "Evgenii Onegin"', *Literatura v shkole* 2 (1974)

Lebedeva, O.B., 'Iz kommentariev k "Evgeniu Oneginu"... I kudri chernye do plech', *Vremennik pushkinskoi komissii*, 24 (Leningrad, 1991), 155-62

Lerner, N.O., 'Iz desiatoi (sozhzhennoi) glavy "Evgeniia Onegina"', in *A.S. Pushkin. Sochineniia* (ed. S.A. Vengerov) (Petersburg, 1915), vol. 6

———'Novye priobreteniia pushkinshogo teksta i dopolneniia. Iz desiatoi (sozhzhennoi) glavy "Evgeniia Onegina"', in *Pushkin*, vi (Brockhaus-Efron, 1915)

———'Pushkinologicheskie etiudy. Zametki na poliakh "Evgeniia Onegina"', *Zvenia* 5 (1935), 60-2

Lotman, Iu., 'K evoliutsii postroeniia kharakterov v romane "Evgenii Onegin", *Pushkin: Issledovaniia i materialy* 3 (Moscow, ANSSR, 1960), 131-73

———'Khudozhestvennaia struktura "Evgenii Onegina", *Trudy po russkoi i slavianskoi filologii* 9 (Tartu) (1966), 5-22

———'K strukture dialogicheskogo teksta v poemakh Pushkina', in *Pushkin i ego sovremenniki* (ed,. E. A, Maimin) (Pskov, LGPI, 1970), 101-10

———*Roman v stikhakh Pushkina 'Evgenii Onegin'. Spetskurs, vvodnye lektsii v izuchenie teksta* (Tartu, Tartuskii gosudarstvennyi universitet, 1975)

———'Smert' kak problema siuzheta', *Literary Tradition and Practice in Russian Culture. Papers from an International Conference on the Occasion of the Seventieth Birthday of Yury Mikhailovich Lotman* in (eds. V. Polukhina, J. Andrew & R. Reid) (Amsterdam/ Atlanta, Rodopi; Series in Slavic Literature and Poetics, 1993), 1-15

———*Pushkin* (St. Petersburg, Iskusstvo-SPB, 1995)

Maimin, E.A., *Pushkin. Zhizn' i tvorchestvo* (Moscow, Nauka. 1981)

Makhov, A.E., '"Magicheskii kristal" A.S. Pushkina i "Volshebnyi khrustalek" N.M. Konshina', *Russkaia rech'*, 3 (1991), 3-7

Makogonenko, G.P., *Roman Pushkina 'Evgenii Onegin'* (Moscow, Goslitizdat, 1963)

Marchenko, V.N. (N. Narokov), 'Kalendar' "Evgeniia Onegina"', *Vozrozhdenie* 62 (1957), 53-62

Markovich, V., 'O mifologicheskom podtekste sna Tat'iany', in *Boldinskie chteniia* (Gor'kii, 1981)

Matsapura, V.I., 'Rabota A.S. Pushkina na obrazom Onegina: Iz nabliudeniia za chernovymi variantami romana v stikhakh', *Voprosy russkoi literatury: Respublikanskii mezhvedomstvennyi nauchnyi sbornik* 52 (1987), 67-75

———'Podrazhaniia "Evgeniiu Oneginu" na Ukraine (20-40e gody XIX)', *Voprosy russkoi literatury: Respublikanskii mezhvedomstvennyi nauchnyi sbornik* 2 (56) (1990), 113-21

Meilakh, B., *A.S. Pushkin* (M-L., Akademiia nauk, 1949)

Mikhailova, N.I., 'Roman "Evgenii Onegin" i oratorskaia kul'tura pervoi treti XIX v', in *Pushkin. Issledovaniia i materialy*, 13 (1989), 45-62

———'Oneginskaia entsiklopediia: Ot zamysla k vosploscheniiu', *Oktiabr'* 2 (1995), 162-76

Mil'chiner, V. & Nemzer, A., 'Roman, kotoryi mozhet udivit", (review) *Voprosy literatury* (Rockville), 9 (1981), 256-64

Modzalevskii, B.L., 'Biblioteka Pushkina: Bibliograficheskoe opisanie', in *Pushkin i ego sovremenniki* 9-10 (St. Petersburg, Ak. Nauk, 1910), 1-442

Moiseev, A.I., 'Kak chitalsia 6-i stikh 33-i strofy 2-i glavy "Evgeniia Onegina"', *Filologicheskie nauki* 2 (1975)

Morozov, P., 'Shifrovannoe stikhotvorenie Pushkina', in *Pushkin i ego sovremenniki* iv (1910), 1-12

Murav'eva, I., 'Vot moi Onegin', *Grani*, 144 (1987), 63-83

Mur'ianov, M.F., 'Portret Lenskogo v "Evgenii Onegine"', *Wiener Slavistische Jahrbüch*, 40 (1994), 75-90

Nedzvetskii, V.A., 'Prozaizatsiia poemy kak put' "eposu novogo mira": "Evgenii Onegin" A.S. Pushkina', *Vestnik Moskovskogo Universiteta. Seriia 9, Filologiia* 9 (1995), 22-33

Nepomniashchii, V.S., 'Nachalo bol'shogo stikhotvoreniia: *Evgenii Onegin* v tvorcheskoi biografii Pushkina, opyt analiza pervoi glavy', *Voprosy literatury* 6 (1982), 124-70

Nikulina, G., 'Za pushkinskoi strokoi', *Literaturnoe obozrenie,* 6 (1985), 99-101

Nishikov, Iu. M., 'Onegin i Tat'iana', *Filologicheskie nauki* 3 (1972), 16-26

———*Istoricheskii i bytovoi fon romana Pushkina "Evgenii Onegin", uchebnoe posobie* (Kalinin, Kalininskii gos. universitet, 1980)

———*Kontsepsiia geroia v romane Pushkina "Evgenii Onegin", uchebnoe posobie* (Kalinin, Kalininskii gos. universitet, 1982)

———'Khudozhestvennoe vremia v "Evgenii Onegine" A.S. Pushkina', *Filologicheskie nauki* 5 (1984), 9-14

———'"Evgenii Onegin": Geroi i istoriia: Etapy stanovleniia istorizma v pushkinskom romane', *Izvestiia Akademii Nauk, Seriiia literatury i iazyka*, 50, No. 4 (1991), 314-27

Ovsianiko-Kulikovskii, D. N., *Voprosy psikhologii tvorchestva* (StP., Izd. D.E. Zhukovskogo, 1902), 1-76

———*Pushkin* (St. Petersburg, 1912), 85-113

———*Istoriia russkoi intelligentsii: Itogi russkoi khudozhestvennoi literatury XIX v-a.* (St. Petersburg, 1914), 70-90

Pugaev, V. V., 'Onegin-dekabrist ili Onegin "chaadaevets"?: K sporam o X glave "Evgeniia Onegina"', *Studia Slavica Academiae Scientarium Hungaricae*, 37, Nos. 1-4 (1991-2), 273-85

Pushkin: Itogi i problemy izucheniia (Leningrad, Nauka, 1966)

Pushkin v vospominaniiakh sovremennikov (Moscow, Khudozhestvennaia literatura, 1974)

Reiser, S.A., 'K chteniiu 6-ogo stikha 33-i strofy 2-i glavy "Evgeniia Onegina", *Filologicheskie nauki* 3 (1974)

———'Eshche raz o chtenii 6-ogo stikha 33-i strofy 2-i glavy "Evgeniia Onegina", *Filologicheskie nauki* 2 (1975)

Samarin, M., 'Iz mazginaliy k "Yevgeniyu Oneginu", *Naukovye zapiski naukovo-doslidochoi kafedry istorii ukrainskoi kul'tury 6* (1927), 307-14

Sandomirskii, S., *Taina "Onegina": Obrazy i idei romana A.S. Pushkina* (Moscow, Respekt, 1992)

Semenko, I.M., 'O roli obraza "avtora" v "Evgenii Onegine", *Trudy Leningradskogo bibliotechnogo instituta im. N. K. Krupskoi* 2 (1957), 127-46

———'Evoliutsiia Onegina', *Russkaia literatura* 2 (1960), 111-28

Shatalov, S.E., *Geroi romana A.S. Pushkina Evgenii Onegin* (Moscow, Prosveshchenie, 1986)

Shklovskii, V., '"Evgenii Onegin" Pushkin i Stern', in *Ocherki po poetike Pushkina* (Berlin, Epokha, 1923), 197-220

Sidiakov, L.S., '"Evgenii Onegin" i nezavershennaia proza Pushkina 1828-1830 godov', in *Problemy pushkinovedeniia: Sbornik nauchnykh trud* (L., G. ped. inst.im. A.N. Gertsena, 1975), 28-39

———'"Evgenii Onegin" i zamysel "Svetskoi povesti'" 30x godov XIX v. K kharakteristike Onegina v sed'moi glave romana', in *Zamysel, trud, voploshchenie* (ed. V.I. Kuleshov) (Moscow, MGU, 1977), 118-24

———'"Evgenii Onegin" i "Arap Petra Velikogo"', *in Problemy pushkinovedeniia: Sbornik nauchnykh trudov* (Riga, LGU, 1983), 16-22

Simonov, K., 'Aleksandr Sergeevich Pushkin', in *A.S. Pushkin v russkoi kritike* (Moscow, Khudozhestvennaia literatura, 1953), 577-608

Siniavskii, A., (Abram Tertz), *Progulki s Pushkinym* (London, Overseas Publications Interchange, 1975)

Sipovskii, V., 'Onegin, Lenskii i Tat'iana', in *Pushkin. Zhizn' i tvorchestvo* (Petersburg, 1907), 571-8

Skachkova, O.N., 'Peisazh v lirike A.S. Pushkina i v romane Evgenii Onegin", *Wisenschaftliche Zeitschrift der Wilhelm-Pieck-Universität*, 32, No 6 (1983), 17-20

———'Druzheskoe poslanie A.S. Pushkina i "Evgenii Onegin"', in *Problemy pushkinovedeniia: Sbornik nauchnykh trudov* (Riga, LGU, 1983), 5-15

Slominskii, A., *Masterstvo Pushkina* (Moscow, 1959)

Sokolov, D.N., 'Po povodu shifrovannogo stikhotvoreniia Pushkina', in *Pushkin i ego sovremennki* (Petersburg, Ross. gos. akad. tip., 1922)

Solovei, N. Ia., *Roman A.S. Pushkina "Evgenii Onegin"* (Moscow, Vysshaia shkola, 1981)

Solov'eva, V.S., 'Sravneniia v romane A.S. Pushkina "Evgenii Onegin"', *Russkii iazyk v shkole* 3 (1989), 73-8

Stilman, L.N., 'Problemy literaturnykh zhanrov i traditsii v "Evgenii Onegine" Pushkina', in *American Contributions to the Fourth International Congress of Slavists* (Hague, Mouton, 1958), 321-67

Stil' i iazyk Pushkina (ed. K.A. Alaverdov) (Moscow, Uchpedgiz, 1937)

Tamarchenko, D.E., *Iz istorii russkogo klassicheskogo romana: Pushkin, Lermontov, Gogol'* (Moscow-Leningrad, AN SSR, 1961), 18-58

Tarkhov, A.E., 'Kalendar' "Evgeniia Onegina", *Znanie-sila* 9 (1974), 30-3

Tarkhova, A., 'Vstupitel'naia stat'ia' in A.S. Pushkin, *Evgenii Onegin* (Moscow, Khudozhestvennaia literatura, 1978)

Toibin, I.M., '"Evgenii Onegin": poeziia i istoriia', in *Pushkin. Issledovaniia i materialy* ix (L., 1979), 83-99

Tomashevskii, B., 'Ritmika chetyrekhstopnogo iamba po nabliudeniiam nad stikhom "Evgenii Onegina", in *Pushkin i ego sovremenniki* (Petrograd, 1918), 144-87

———'Desiataia glava "Evgeniia Onegina", *Literaturnoe nasledstvo* 16-18 (1934), 378-420

———*Pushkin: Kniga vtoraia* (Moscow-Leningrad, AN SSR, 1961), 444-76

Tschudakow, A., (Chudakov, A.) 'O strukture personazha geroia "Evgeniia Onegina"', in *Arion: Jahrbuch der Deutschen Pushkin-Gesellschaft* (Bonn, 1989), 263-7

Turbin, V.N., 'Romanist i roman', in his *Pushkin, Gogol, Lermontov* (Moscow, Proshveshchenie, 1978), 177-90

———'Onegin i Snegina: K probleme traditisii v poezii', *Oktiabr'* 4 (1983), 187-92

———'"On vidit bashnuiu Godunova...". Motivy i obrazy dramy A.S. Pushkina "Boris Godunov" v romane "Evgenii Onegin"', *Vestnik moskovskogo universiteta. Seriia 9, Filologiia*, 9, No. 3 (1987), 3-7

———'K probleme imeni sobstvennogo v romane A.S. Pushkina *Evgenii Onegin*', *Russian Literature* 24-3 (1988), 433-50

———'Uzheli slovo naideno?' (response to V. Kozhevnikov), *Novyi mir* 6 (1988), 266-8

———'Vospriatiie i interpretatisiia Lermontovym zhanrovoi struktury romana Pushkina "Evgenii Onegina", *Vestnik Moskovskogo Universiteta. Seriia 9, Filologiia*, 9 (1989), 17-27

———'Evgenii Onegin i *M'y*' (sic), *The Pushkin Journal* 1, No. 2 (1993), 197-212

———*Nezadolgo do Vodoleia, sb. statei* (Moscow, Radiks, 1994)

———*Poetika romana A.S. Pushkina "Evgenii Onegin"* (Moscow, Moscow University, 1996)

Tynianov, Iu. N., *Problema stikhotvornogo iazyka* (Leningrad, Akademiia, 1924)

———*Arkhaisty i Pushkin* (Leningrad, 1929), 87-227

———*Poetika, istoriia literatury, kino* (Moscow, Nauka, 1977), 52-77

Vickery, W.N., 'Parellelizm v literaturnom razvitii Bairona i Pushkina', *in American Contributions to the Fifth International Congress of Slavists* (Hague, Mouton, 1963), 371-401

Vilenchuk, B.A., '"Russkii N" sredi abbreviatur "Evgeniia Onegina"', *Russkaia literatura* 2 (1986)

Vinogradov, I., 'Put' Pushkina k realizmu', *Literaturnoe nasledstvo* 16-18 (1934), 49-90

———'O stile Pushkina', *Literaturnoe nasledstvo* 16-18 (1934), 135-214

———*Iazyk Pushkina: Pushkin i istoriia russkogo literaturnogo iazyka* (Moscow-Leningrad, Academia, 1935)

——— *Stil' Pushkina* (Moscow, Ogiz, 1941)

———'Stil' i kompozitsiia pervoi glavy "Evgeniia Onegina"', *Russkii iazyk v shkole* 4 (1966), 3-21

Vinokur, G., 'Slovo i stikh v "Evgenii Onegine", in *Pushkin: Sbornik statei* (ed. A., Egolin) (Moscow, Goslitizdat, 1941), 155-213

'Vtoraia mezhdunarodnaia pushkinskaia konferentsiia', *Russkaia literatura* 3 (1993), 209-20

Zalygin, S., 'Pamiati Pushkina', *Literaturnaia gazeta* 11 February, 1987, p.4.

Zhirmunskii, B.N., *Bairon i Pushkin* (Leningrad, Academia, 1924)

4. Secondary literature (languages other than Russian)

Akhmatova, A., 'Benjamin Constant's *Adolphe* in the Work of Pushkin', *Russian Literature Triquarterly* 10 (1974), 157-79

Barran, T., 'Who Killed Lensky?: The Narrator as Assassin in *Eugene Onegin'*, in *Selected Proceedings of the Kentucky Foreign Language Conference: Slavic Section, 1987-88*, v, No. 1 (1987), 7-15

Bayley, J., *Pushkin: A Comparative Commentary* (Cambridge, Cambridge University Press, 1971)

Bethea, D., *Pushkin Today* (ed.) (Bloomington, Indiana University Press, 1993)

Borland, H., 'Theories and Problems of Translation with Special Reference to Pushkin's Novel in Verse, *Eugene Onegin'*, in *Problemy perevoda* (Melbourne, Melbourne University, undated), 1-32

Boyd, A.F., 'The Master and the Source: Alexander Pushkin and *Eugene Onegin'* in his *Aspects of the Russian Novel* (N.J., Rowman and Littlefield, 1972), 1-23

Briggs, A.D.P., *Eugene Onegin* (Cambridge, CUP, Landmarks of World Literature Series, 1992)

———*Alexander Pushkin. A Critical Study* (Beckenham, Croom Helm, 1983)

———'The Blasphemous Masterpiece: Tchaikovsky's Adaptation of *Eugene Onegin*' (Belfast, Queen's University, 1995)

Brown, W.E., *A History of Russian Literature of the Romantic Period*, iii, (Ann Arbor, Ardis, 1986)

Burgin, D.L., 'Tatiana Larina's *Letter to Onegin*, or *La Plume Criminelle'*, *Essays in Poetics* 19, No. 2 (1991), 12-23

Busch, U., 'Alexander Pushkin, Jevgenij Onegin', in Zelinsky, B., *Der russische Roman* (Düsseldorf, Bagel, 1979), 47-69

Clayton, J.D., 'The Epigraph of *Eugene Onegin*: A Hypothesis', *Canadian Slavonic Studies* 2 (1971), 226-33

———'Emblematic and Iconographic Patterns in Pushkin's *Eugene Onegin*: A Shakespearean Ghost?', *Germano-Slavica* 1: 6 (1975), 53-66

———'Considérations sur la chronologie interne de *Evgenii Onegin*', *Canadian Slavonic Papers*, XXI: 4 (1979), 479-88

———'Pushkin, Faust and the Demons', *Germano-Slavica* III:3 (1980), 165-87

———'New Directions in Soviet Criticism on *Evgenii Onegin*', *Canadian Slavonic Papers* XXII (1980), 208-19

———'Evgenij Onegin: Symbolism of Time and Space', *Russian Language Journal* XXV, No. 120 (1981), 43-58

———*Ice and Flame. Aleksandr Pushkin's Eugene Onegin* (Toronto, University of Toronto Press, 1985)

———'Towards a feminist reading of *Evgenii Onegin*', *Canadian Slavonic Papers* xxix (1987), 255-65

Clipper-Sethi, R., 'A Lesson for Novelists: or, The Dramatic Structure of *Evgenij Onegin'*, *Russian Literature* xiv-xvi (1983), 397-411

Crookes, D.Z., 'A Contextual Study of the Musical Instruments in Pushkin's Yevgeny Onegin', *New Zealand Slavonic Journal* (1984), 1-13

de Haard, E., 'On the Narrative Structure of Evgenij Onegin', *Russian Literature* 36-4 (1989), 451-67

Dolinin, A., 'Eugene Onegin', in V. Alexandrov (ed.) *The Garland Companion to Vladimir Nabokov* (New York, Garland, 1995), 117-30

Downey, N.E., *The Garden in the Graveyard: Memory in Pushkin's 'Evgeny Onegin'*, (unpublished dissertation, Brown University, 1995) (abstract in *Dissertation Abstracts International,* 55, No. 9, March 1995, 285A-59A)

Driver, S., *Pushkin. Literature and Social Ideas* (New York, Columbia University Press, 1989)

Dvinin, V., '*Reader's letter*: Pushkin's Tatyana and the Sceptic: A Study in Cynicism', *New Zealand Slavonic Journal* 2 (1975), 85-6

Eidel'man, N., '*Evgenii Onegin*: The mystery of the tenth chaper', *Soviet Studies in Literature* xi, No. 1 (Winter, 1974-5), 8-15

Emerson, C., 'Tatiana' in *A Plot of her Own. The Female Protagonist in Russian Literature* (ed. S. Hoisington) (Evanston, Northwestern UP, 1995)

Fanger, D., 'Influence and Tradition in the Russian Novel', in *The Russian Novel from Pushkin to Pasternak* (ed. J. Garrard) (Yale, Yale University Press, 1983), 29-50

Fennell, J., *Nineteenth-century Russian Literature: Studies of Ten Russian Writers* (London, 1973)

Forsyth, J., 'Pisarev, Belinsky and *Yevgeniy Onegin*', *Slavonic and East European Review* 48 (1970), 451-92

Franklin, S., 'Novels Without End: Notes on "Eugene Onegin" and "Dead Souls"', *Modern Language Review* 79, No. 2 (1984), 372-83

Freeborn, R., *The Rise of the Russian Novel from 'Eugene Onegin' to 'War and Peace'* (Cambridge, Cambridge University Press, 1973), 13-68

Garrard, J., 'Corresponding Heroines in "Don Juan" and "Evgenii Onegin"', *Slavonic and East European Review* 73, No. 3 (1995), 428-48

Gershenzon, 'Dreams in Pushkin', *Russian Literature Triquarterly* 24 (Spring, 1990), 163-76

Gibian, G,. 'Narrative Technique and Realism: *Evgenii Onegin* and *Madame Bovary*', *Langue et littérature* (1962), p. 339

Gifford, H., *The Novel in Russia* (London, Hutchinson, 1964), 15-20

Goscilo, H., 'Multiple Texts in *Eugene Onegin*: A Preliminary Examination', *Russian Literature Triquarterly* 24 (Spring, 1990), 271-86

Greenleaf, M., 'Romantic Irony in *Eugene Onegin*' in her *Pushkin and Romantic Fashion* (Stanford, Stanford University Press, 1994)

Gregg, L., 'Slava Snabokovu', *Russian Literature Triquarterly* 3 (1972) 313-29

Gregg, R.A., 'Tatyana's Two Dreams: The Unwanted Spouse and the Demonic Lover', *Slavonic and East European Review* 48 (1970), 492-505

———'Rhetoric in Tat'iana's last speech', *Slavic and East European Journal* 25, No. 1 (1981), 1-12

———'Pushkin's Narratives and the Hex of Darkness', *Slavic Review* 48, No. 4 (Winter, 1989), 547-57 (553-5)

———Stanza and Plot in *Evgenii Onegin*: A Symbiosis?', *Slavonic and East European Review*, 72, No. 4 (October, 1994), 609-21

Grübel, R., 'Convention and Innovation of Aesthetic Value: The Russian Reception of Aleksandr Puskin', in Theo D'haen, Rainer Grübel & Helmut Lethen, (eds.), *Convention and Innovation in Literature* (Amsterdam/Philadelphia, Benjamins, 1989), 181-224

Gustafson, R.F., 'The Metaphor of the Seasons in Evgenij Onegin', *Slavic and East European Journal* 6, No. 1 (1962), 6-20

Hellberg, E.F., 'Kak v zerkale: Gadanie i son Tat'iany', *Studia Slavica Finlandensia* 6 (1989), 1-19

Hielscher, K., *A.S. Puskins Versepik. Autoren-, Ich- und Erzählstruktur* (München, Otto Sagner, 1966), 118-23

Hoisington, S.S., '*Eugene Onegin*: An Inverted Byronic Poem', *Comparative Literature* 27, No. 2 (1975), 136-52

———'The Hierarchy of Narratees in *Eugene Onegin*', *Canadian-American Slavic Studies* 10 (1976), 242-9

———'*Eugene Onegin*: Product of or Challenge to *Adolphe*', *Comparative Literature Studies* 14 (1977), 205-13

———'Parody in *Evgenii Onegin*: Lenskii's Lament', *Canadian Slavonic Papers*, Nos. 2-3 (June-September, 1987), 266-78

Jakobson, R., *Pushkin and His Sculptural Myth* (Hague, Mouton, 1975)

Johnson, D. Barton, 'Nabokov's *Ada* and Pushkin's *Eugene Onegin*', *Slavic and East European Journal* 15, No. 3 (1971), 316-23

Jones, R.D., 'Linguistic and Metrical Constraints in Verse: Iambic and Trochaic Tetramaters of Pushkin', in *Linguistic and Literary Studies in Honor of Archibald A. Hill iv: Linguistics and Literature; Sociolinguistics and Applied Linguistics* (eds. M. Jazayery, E. Polome & W. Winter) (Hague, Mouton, 1979, 87-101

Katz, M.R., 'Dreams in Pushkin', *California Slavic Studies* xi (1980), 71-103 (pp. 91-102)

———'Love and Marriage in Pushkin's *Evgenii Onegin*', *Oxford Slavonic Papers* (1984), 77-89

Kiray, G., 'Siuzhet i dialog v *Evgenii Onegine* Pushkina, *Shineli* Gogolia i *Besakh* Dostoevskogo', *Studia Rossica Posnaniensa*, 20 (1988), 3-15

Kluge, R-D., 'Belinskij und Dostoevskij um Streit um Pushkins Tat′jana', *Zeitschrift für Slawistik,* 32, No. 2 (1987), 238-50

Komarovsky, J., '*Eugen Onegin* A.S. Pushkina v polemike s sentimentalnym romanom', *Slovica Slavaca*, 23, No. 4 (1988), 352-65

Lavrin, J., *Pushkin and Russian Literature* (New York, Russell & Russell, 1947), 119-139

Levitt, M.C., *Russian Literary Politics and the Pushkin Celebration of 1880* (Ithaca, Cornell University Press, 1989)

———'Pushkin Pro Semiosis: The Dialectic of the Sign in Canto One of *Evgenii Onegin*', *Russian Literature* 34-4 (1993), 439-50

Little, T.E., 'Pushkin's Tatyana and Onegin: A Study in Irony', *New Zealand Slavonic Journal*, 1 (1975), 19-28

Lo Gatto, E., 'L'*Onegin* come "diario lirico" di Pushkin', *Analecta Slavica: A Slavonic Miscellany* (Amsterdam, De Bezige Bij, 1955), 91-108

———E., 'Su di un problema formale dell'*Onegin*', *Ricerche Slavistische* 6 (1958), 41-83

———E., 'Sull'elemento lirico-autobiografico nell'*Evgenij Onegine* di Pushkin', in *Studies in Russian and Polish Literature in Honor of Waclaw Lednicki* (ed. Z. Folejewski) (S-Gravenhage, Mouton, 1962), 105-113

Lotman, Ju., 'Point of View in a Text', *New Literary History* 6 (1975), 339-52

Markstein, E., 'Auf der Süche nach dem deutschen Onegin', *Wiener Slawistischer Almanach*, 10 (1982), 137-49

Martinez, L., 'Les figures du temps dans *Evgenij Onegin'*, *Revue des Études slaves*, 59, Nos. 1-2 (1987), 21-44

Matlaw, R., 'The Dream in *Evgeny Onegin*, with a Note on *Gore ot uma*', *Slavonic and East European Journal* 37 (1959), 487-503

McLean, H., 'The Tone(s) of Evgenij Onegin', *California Slavic Studies* 6 (1971), 3-15

Meijer. J.M., 'The Digressions in Evgenij Onegin', in *Dutch Contributions to the Sixth International Congress of Slavists* (ed. A.G.F. van Holk) (Hague, Mouton, 1968), 122-52

Meyer, P., 'Nabokov's *Lolita* and Pushkin's *Onegin*: McAdam, McEve and McFate', in Gibian, G. & Parker, S. (eds.), *The Achievements of Vladimir Nabokov: Essays, Studies, Reminiscences and Stories from the Cornell Nabokov Festival* (Ithaca, Center for International Studies, Cornell University, 1984), 179-211

Miller, T., & Boyd, M.S. (tr.), 'Lermontov Reads *Eugene Onegin*', *The Russian Review*, 53, No. 1 (1994), 59-66

Millet-Gerard, D., 'Dandys et "grandes coquettes" de Pouchkine et Balzac et Lermontov', *L'Année Balzacienne*, 14 (1993), 41-63

Mirskii, D.S., *Pushkin* (New York, Dutton, 1926/reprinted 1963)

Mitchell, S., 'The Digressions of *Yevgeniy Onegin*: Apropos of Some Essays by Ettore Lo Gatto', *Slavonic and East European Review* 44 (1966), 51-65

Mitchell, S., 'Tatiana's Reading', *Forum for Modern Language Studies*, 4, No. 1 (January, 1968), 1-21

Mondry, H., *The Evaluation of Ideological Trends in Recent Soviet Literary Scholarships* (München, Otto Sagner, 1990)

Müller, L., 'Shicksal und Liebe in "Jewgenij Onegin"', *So Lange Dichte Leben* (Krefeld, 1949)

———'Tatjanas Traum', *Die Welt der Slawen* 7 (1962), 387-94

Nesaule, W., 'Tat'jana's dream in Pushkin's *Evgenij Onegin*', *Indiana Slavic Studies* 4 (1968), 119-24

O'Bell, L., 'In Pushkin's Library', *Canadian-American Slavonic Studies* 26, No. 2 (Summer, 1982), 207-26

Peer, L.H., 'Pushkin and Goethe Again: Lensky's Character', *Papers on Language and Literature* 5 (1969), 267-72

Picchio, R., 'Dante and Malfilâtre as Literary Sources of Tat'iana's Erotic Dream (Notes on the Third Chapter of Pushkin's *Evgenij Onegin*', *in Aleksander Pushkin: A Symposium on the 175th Anniversary of His Birth* (New York, New York University Press, 1976), 42-55

Rancour-Laferrière, D., 'Pushkin's Still Unravished Bride: A Psychoanalytic Study of Tat'iana's Dream', *Russian literature* 25-2 (1989), 215-49

Reeve, F.D., *The Russian Novel* (New York, McGraw, 1966), 14-44

Riggan, W., '*Werther, Adolphe* and *Eugene Onegin*: The Decline of the Hero of Sensibility', *Research Studies* (Washington State University) 41 (1973), 252-67

Roosevelt, P.R., 'Tatiana's Garden: Noble Sensibilities and Estate Park Design in the Romantic Era', *Slavic Review* 49, No. 3 (Fall, 1990), 335-49 (pp. 347-50)

Rosengrant, J., 'Nabokov, Onegin, and the Theory of Translation', *Slavic and East European Journal*, 38, No. 1 (1994), 13-32

Rosza, M., 'Die Veranderugen von Onegins Gestalt in den Übersetzungen von Freidrich Bodenstedt und Karoly Berczy', *Studia Slavica*, 38, Nos. 3-4 (1993), 353-64

Russian Views of Pushkin (eds. D.J. Richards & C.R.S. Cockrell) (Oxford, Meeuws, 1976)

Ryan, W.F., & Wigzell, F., 'Gullible Girls and Dreadful dreams. Zhukovskii, Pushkin and Popular Divination', *Slavonic and East European Review*, 70, No. 4 (October, 1992), 647-69)

Sandler, S., *Distant Pleasures: Alexander Pushkin and the Writing of Exile* (Stanford, Stanford University Press, 1989)

———'Sex, Death and Nation in the Strolls with Pushkin Controversy', *Slavic Review* 51, No. 2 (Summer, 1992), 294-308

Scheffler, L., *Das erotische Sujet in Pushkins Dichtung* (Munich, Wilhelm Fink, 1967), 154-200

Scherr, B.P., *Russian Poetry* (Berkely, University of California Press, 1986), 235-7

Schmidgall, G., *Literature as Opera* (New York, OUP, 1977)

Schmidt, P., 'Pushkin and Istomina – ballet in nineteenth-century Russia', *Dance Research Journal* 2 (1988), 3-7

———'A Winter Feast', *Parnassus: Poetry in Review* 16, No. 1 (1990), 16-30

Seehase, I., 'Onegin: Ein Stein des Anstosses: Aus der schwierigen Rezeptionsgeschichte einer literarischen Gestalt', *Zeitschrift für Slawistik* 29, No. 4 (1984), 522-34

Setschkareff, V., *Alexander Puschkin: Sein Leben und Sein Werk* (Wiesbaden, Otto Harrassowitz, 1963)

Shaw, J.T., 'Recent Soviet Scholarly Books on Pushkin: A Review Article', *Slavic and East European Journal* 10, No. 1 (1966), 64-84

———'The Problem of Unity of Author-Narrator's Stance in *Pushkin's Evgenij Onegin*', *Russian Language Journal* 35, No. 120 (1981), 25-42

———*Pushkin's Poetics of the Unexpected. The nonrhymed lines in the rhymed poetry and the rhymed lines in the nonrhymed poetry* (Columbus, Slavica, 1993)

Simmons, E.J., 'English Translations of *Eugene Onegin*', *Slavonic and East European Review* xvii, No. 49 (1938) , 198-209

Skovajasa, K.J., *Vladimir Nabokov's 'Eugene Onegin'. A Critical Study* (Phd dissertation, University of Oregon, unpublished, 1971)

Smith, G.S., 'Notes on Prosody', in *The Garland Companion to Vladimir Nabokov* (ed. V. Alexandrov) (New York, Garland, 1995), 561-66

Städtke, K., 'Zum Problem der deutschen Puskin-Rezeption', *Zeitschrift für Slawistik*, 32, No. 1 (1987), 23-9

———'Literarischer Text und Salonkultur. Anmerkungen zu Pushkins Vers-roman "Eugen Onegin"', in *Arion. Jahrbuch der Deutschen Pushkin-Gesellschaft* (Bonn, 1989), 239-52

Tangl, E., 'Tatjanas Traum', *Zeitschrift fur slavische Philologie* 25 (1956), 230-60

Tempest, R., 'The Girl on the Hill: Parallel Structures in *Pride and Prejudice* and *Eugene Onegin'*, *Elementa: Journal of Slavic Studies and Comparative Cultural Semiotics*, 1, No. 2 (1993), 197-213

The Cambridge History of Russian Literature (ed. C. Moser) (Cambridge, CUP, 1992)

Todd, W.M., *The Familiar Letter as a Literary Genre in the Age of Pushkin* (Princeton, Princeton University Press, 1976)

———'Eugene Onegin: Life's Novel' in *Literature and Society in Imperial Russia 1800-1914* (ed. W.M. Todd) (Stanford, 1978), 214-17; also as 'Eugene Onegin: Life's Novel', in his *Fiction and Society in the Age of Pushkin* (Cambridge, Mass., 1986), 106-136

———'The Russian Terpsichore's Soul-Filled Flight: Dance Themes in *Eugene Onegin*', in *Pushkin Today* (ed. D. Bethea) (Bloomington, Indiana UP., 1993), 13-30

Ueland, C., 'Viacheslav Ivanov's Pushkin: Thematic and Prosodic Echoes *of Evgenii Onegin* in *Mladenchestvo*', *in Mythologies of Russian Modernism: From the Golden Age to the Silver Age* (eds. B. Gasparov, R. Hughes, I. Paperno & E. Naiman) (Berkeley, University of California Press, 1992), 337-55

Vickery, W. N., 'Byron's *Don Juan* and Pushkin's *Evgenij Onegin*: The Question of Parallelism', *Indiana Slavic Studies* 4 (1968), 181-91

———*Alexander Pushkin* (New York, Twayne Publishers, 1970), 102-29

Warner, R.V., *The Sviatki folk ritual in Pushkin's Evgenii Onegin and Tolstoy's War and Peace: A multi-level performance* (MA thesis, Ohio State University, 1995)

Weil, I., 'Onegin's Echo', *Russian Literature Triquarterly* 10 (1974), 260-73

Weintraub, W., 'Norwid's "Spartacus" and the "Onegin" Stanza', *Harvard Slavic Studies* 2 (1954), 271-86

Wilson, E., '*Evgenii Onegin*: In Honour of Pushkin 1799-1837', *New Republic* 89 (9 December, 1936), 165-71

______*The Triple Thinkers* (London, John Lehman, 1952)

______'The strange case of Pushkin and Nabokov', in *A Window on Russia* (London, 1972), 209-37

Wollf, M. D. 'Romanticism Unmasked: Lexical Irony in Aleksandr Puskin's *Evgenij Onegin*', in *Convention and Innovation in Literature* (eds. T. D'haen, R. Grübel & H. Lethen) (Amsterdam/Philadelphia, Benjamins, 1989), 361-88

Woodward, J.B., 'The principle of contradictions in *Yevgeniy Onegin*', *Slavonic and East European Review* 60 (1982), 25-43

Worth, D.S., 'Grammatical Rhyme Types in *Evgenij Onegin*' in *Alexander Pushkin Symposium II* (eds. A. Kodjak, K. Pomorska, K. Taranovsky) (Columbus, Slavica, 1980), 39-48

———'Rhyme Enrichment in *Evgenii Onegin*', in *Miscellanea Slavica: To Honour the Memory of Jan M. Meijer* (Amsterdam, Rodopi, 1983), pp. 535-42

Zekulin, N.G., '*Evgenii Onegin*: The Art of Adaptation, Novel to Opera', *Canadian Slavonic Papers*, 29 Nos. 2-3 (1987), 279-91

Appendix

Евгений Онегин 1: 1

1 2 3 4
«Мой дя́д/я са́м/ых че́ст/ных пра́вил,

Когда́/ же в шу́/тку за/немо́г,

Он ув/ажа́ть/ себя́/ заста́вил

И лу́/чше вы́/думать/ не мог.

Его́/ приме́р/ други́м/ нау́ка;

Но, бо́/же мо́й/, кака́/я ску́ка

С больны́м/ сиде́ть/ и де́нь/ и но́чь,

Не отх/одя́/ ни ша́/гу прочь!

Како́/е ни́з/кое/ кова́рство

Полу/живо́г/о заб/авля́ть,

Ему́/ поду́ш/ки поп/равля́ть,

Печа́ль/но под/носи́ть/ лека́р/ство,

Вздыха́ть/ и ду́м/ать про/ себя́:

Когда́/ же чёрт/ возьмёт/ тебя́?»

Index